W9-BYB-526

BE MY
Refuge,
LORD

BOB & EMILIE BARNES

HARVEST HOUSE PUBLISHERS

EUGENE, OREGON

Unless otherwise indicated, all Scripture quotations are taken from the New American Standard Bible®, © 1960, 1962, 1963, 1968, 1971, 1972, 1973, 1975, 1977, 1995 by The Lockman Foundation. Used by permission. (www.Lockman.org)

Verses marked NIV are taken from the HOLY BIBLE, NEW INTERNATIONAL VERSION®. NIV®. Copyright © 1973, 1978, 1984 by the International Bible Society. Used by permission of Zondervan. All rights reserved.

Verses marked TLB are taken from *The Living Bible*, Copyright © 1971. Used by permission of Tyndale House Publishers, Inc., Wheaton, IL 60189 USA. All rights reserved.

Verses marked KJV are taken from the King James Version of the Bible.

Verses marked NKJV are taken from the New King James Version. Copyright © 1982 by Thomas Nelson, Inc. Used by permission. All rights reserved.

Verses marked NLT are taken from the *Holy Bible*, New Living Translation, copyright © 1996. Used by permission of Tyndale House Publishers, Inc., Wheaton, IL 60189 USA. All rights reserved.

Every effort has been made to give proper credit for all stories, poems, and quotations. If for any reason proper credit has not been given, please notify the author or publisher and proper notation will be given on future printing.

Cover by Terry Dugan Design, Minneapolis, Minnesota

Cover photo © Shaun Egan / The Image Bank / Getty Images

BE MY REFUGE, LORD
Copyright © 2007 by Bob and Emilie Barnes
Published by Harvest House Publishers
Eugene, Oregon 97402

Library of Congress Cataloging-in-Publication Data

Barnes, Bob, 1933–
  Be my refuge, Lord.
    p. cm.
  ISBN-13: 978-0-7369-1991-3 (pbk.)
  ISBN-10: 0-7369-1991-0 (pbk.)
  1. Bible. O.T. Psalms—Meditations. 2. Suffering—Biblical teaching. I. Barnes, Emilie. II. Title.
  BS1430.6.S8B37 2007
  242'.5—dc22

                                                                2006031306

All rights reserved. No part of this publication may be reproduced, stored in a retrieval system, or transmitted in any form or by any means—electronic, mechanical, digital, photocopy, recording, or any other—except for brief quotations in printed reviews, without the prior permission of the publisher.

Printed in the United States of America

07 08 09 10 11 12 13 14 15 / VP-SK / 12 11 10 9 8 7 6 5 4 3 2 1

A Note from Emilie

This book is dedicated to all of my prayer supporters. Without all of your continual prayers, I would not have had the health to put these thoughts on paper. Your prayers, cards, e-mails, letters, and phone calls have given me the encouragement to live and contribute to the Christian community.

In the past, and especially during my years of illness, Bob and I went to the Psalms for comfort. These thoughts and promises have given me the strength to greet each day with hope.

I appreciate all that you've done for me. I could not have made the journey without your support. May you enjoy reading this book as much as Bob and I have enjoyed writing it for you.

Sharing the Wonder
of the Psalms

~~~

$\mathcal{T}$he Book of Psalms is a collection of songs, laments, and praises. The Jews referred to this book as "The Book of Praises," while the Septuagint entitled it "The Book of Psalms" from the Greek word indicating songs sung to the accompaniment of stringed instruments. This book was the hymnal of the Jewish people.

Of the 150 chapters in Psalms, David is credited with being the author of 73. Various other authors contributed to the book's composition. This book has been a comfort to many people over the centuries. One of the most-read psalms is the Twenty-third. It is also one of the most memorized pieces of literature in the world:

> The Lord is my shepherd, I shall not want. He makes me lie down in green pastures; He leads me beside quiet waters. He restores my soul; He guides me in the paths of righteousness for His name's sake. Even though I walk through the valley of the shadow of death, I fear no evil, for You are with me; Your rod and Your staff, they comfort me. You prepare a table before me in the presence of my enemies; You have anointed my head with oil; my cup overflows. Surely goodness and lovingkindness will follow me all the days of my life, and I will dwell in the house of the Lord forever (Psalm 23:1-6).

Our desire is for this book to be an inspiration when you are downtrodden, stressed, depressed, ill, discouraged, or feeling like you are at the bottom of a pit. The Psalms stimulate a common response in people because we all share in difficult times. The experiences might be different in cause or nature, but the struggles and the doubts are similar. As we pass through these valleys and feel an even greater need to turn to the strength of the Lord and the power of His Word, we can relate to the emotions, longings, pleas, and praises discovered in Psalms.

These scriptures are a means for us to experience our own feelings, and also to encourage us as we ponder God's dealing with us during this difficult time. I have found that no matter what my situation might be, I can turn to the powerful collection of poetry and praises of Psalms and know that a phrase, a prayer, a sentiment will be just the thing to soothe my soul.

The writing of this book has been such an inspiration to us. When we were down, we became lifted up, and when we felt victory, we sang a song of praise.

At the top of each devotion you will see three boxes:

◻ ◻ ◻

Each time you read a meditation, put a check mark in one of the boxes to keep track of what you have studied. You're invited to skip around and choose the reading that seems most suited for the day ahead.

Accompanying each devotion is a prayer to initiate your conversation with God. We encourage the practical application of each day's message with a simple idea for action. You will find that during the day you will have transformed that one action idea into many, and the blessings will just keep multiplying. To close each devotion, we add a bit of "Today's Wisdom" that gives you extra encouragement to carry with you through the day. Through all of these elements, we pray that you will discover a greater intimacy with the Giver of all truth: our Lord.

While we collaborated throughout this writing and devotional journey, the devotions remain as Emilie's thoughts to you. We cannot wait to see how your time in Psalms will inspire your life and remind you that God is eager to embrace His children and bring them through the trials, the joys, and the many adventures life presents. We are honored to walk beside you as you begin.

—Bob and Emilie Barnes

Walking Upright in the Lord

*Blessed is the man who does not walk in the
counsel of the wicked or stand in the way of
sinners or sit in the seat of mockers. But his
delight is in the law of the LORD, and on his
law he meditates day and night. He is like a
tree planted by streams of water, which yields its
fruit in season and whose leaf does not wither.
Whatever he does prospers.*

PSALM 1:1-3 NIV

*O*ne of a person's deepest quests in life is for happiness or the
key to being happy. Everywhere we look, people are searching for
happiness through the jobs they have, the homes they live in, the
toys they play with, the food they eat, and the vacations they take.
But to their amazement, when they finally arrive at what they had
wanted, they often find that happiness has moved and left no for-
warding address.

A poet once said, "Happiness is much more equally divided than
some of us imagine. One man shall possess most of the materials
but little of the thing; another man possesses much of the thing but
very few of the materials."

This tension is one of life's greatest struggles: How do we balance
between things and happiness? In today's passage, we concentrate
on three areas concerning happiness:

1. What to avoid
2. What to concentrate on
3. What a happy person is like

What to Avoid

David warns us not to take advice from the wrong people. Paul in Romans 3:4 states, "Let God be true, and every man a liar." It is important that we seek wise counsel. We cannot be conformed to the world system. Magazines, television, newspapers, and the Internet are not where we gain wisdom.

The bottom line is to have quality friends—friends who have strong character qualities and can provide wisdom in their speech.

What to Concentrate On

We have become so accustomed to the media's fast pace and dissemination of information that we desire all episodes of life to be narrowed down to a few minutes, if not just a few seconds. We lose concentration and patience when a person or situation takes too long.

To counter our lack of concentration, we must learn or relearn to delight and meditate. We go to Scripture with delight, but once we close the Bible and go about our day, do we lose its joy? If we would approach Scripture each day with the intent to hold on to its wisdom and teachings and take them with us into our days, we would see wonderful changes in our attitudes and lives. Psalm 1:2 says we are to delight in the law of the Lord and to meditate on His law day and night.

What a Happy Person Is Like

David describes a blessed person to be like a tree planted by streams of water. We can find happiness when we are grounded near the ever-present source of nourishment and wisdom: God and His Word. A happy person absorbs this refreshment and becomes someone who yields much fruit as he or she works, develops relationships, and serves the Lord. This person does not lose wisdom and passion during trials, but rather embraces God's abundance and prospers.

PRAYER

*F*ather God, I want to be happy in the Lord. I desire to have a balance between the things of this life and a desire to be anchored to You by planting my trees by the streams of water so that I can yield fruit in season. Let me avoid those things I should avoid and concentrate on the things I should concentrate on. Amen.

ACTION

*M*ajor on the major and minor on the minor.

TODAY'S WISDOM

I know Christ dwells within me all the time, guiding me and inspiring me whenever I do or say anything. A light of which I caught no glimmer before comes to me at the very moment when it is needed.

SAINT THERESE OF LISIEUX

You Have a Direct Line

*The Lord has set apart the redeemed
for himself. Therefore he will listen to me and
answer when I call to him.*

PSALM 4:3 TLB

*W*hen my Bob ran a factory-built housing company, he was constantly in meetings with various staff personnel. However he always told me and the children that if we needed to talk to him, we could call him directly and he would be available—no matter what. If I can go directly to my husband, how much greater it is to go to God directly. It is good to be able to call upon God anytime—morning, noon, or night—and know that He will have time for little ol' me. I never get a busy signal or put on hold when I call Him. God is more reliable than dialing 911. Just think: God has given us a direct line. What a privilege to be a child of God! Our Creator is always ready to listen to us.

There have been many times when I have stood at a fork in the road, unsure which path I should take, and I called out to God. In each situation, He gave me clarity of thought, but the final decision was mine.

In this scripture, the promise is that God will always listen to and answer the redeemed. If you are able to call yourself one of His children, you are able to call out to God. He hears your cries.

As we become busy with taking care of our families, ourselves, and the day-to-day business of life, it is so easy to forget our direct line to our Savior. We are blessed to be cared for so deeply that our Maker desires our companionship and communication. He awaits our call.

PRAYER

*F*ather God, I cannot believe that You are interested in me! I'm able to have your private number—day or night You answer my call. What an assurance to know that You care for me. Amen.

ACTION

*C*all God today on His private line.

TODAY'S WISDOM

The Difference

I got up early one morning
and rushed into the day;
I had so much to accomplish
that I didn't have time to pray.

Problems just tumbled about me,
and heavier came each task.
"Why doesn't God help me?" I wondered.
He answered, "You didn't ask."

I wanted to see joy and beauty,
but the day toiled on, gray and bleak;
I wondered why God didn't show me.
He said, "But you didn't seek."

I tried to come into God's presence,
I used all my keys at the lock.
God gently and lovingly chided,
"My child, you didn't knock."

I woke up early this morning,
and paused before entering the day;
I had so much to accomplish
that I had to take time to pray.

GRACE L. NAESSENS

Let Go, Let God

Offer right sacrifices and trust in the LORD.
PSALM 4:5

*E*vangelist Billy Strachan tells of a time when he was sitting in his study, engaged in a serious discussion with a friend, when his young daughter walked into the room holding her jump rope in a tangled mess. She handed the rope to her dad and quietly left. Continuing his intense conversation with his friend, Billy untied the knots in her rope almost without thinking. A few minutes later his daughter returned and said, "Thanks, Daddy," and skipped out to play. Why can't we be like that with our heavenly Father? Why do we work so hard at our own efforts when we can turn our problems over to Him and let Him work them out?

No wonder Jesus loved little children so much. He knew that their simple, uncomplicated lives would be brought to Him in simple faith. We need to approach God in a similar fashion. How many times do we struggle with our everyday situations? As independent people, we tend to try to solve all of our problems by ourselves. When will we learn to put our trust in the Lord?

One very effective way to overcome the stress of life is to search for peace. There is an understanding that all's well when we have an inner peace, a quality of internal rest and calm. In order to experience this kind of peace, we must be willing to release everything to God.

We know that we have real tranquillity when things are chaotic all around us and we can be calm and trust in the Lord. He is the One who calms the storms of our life (and storms will occur—just be ready).

If you are struggling with situations at home, work, school, or church, or if you are in a relationship that needs to be turned over to Jesus for help, let go, let God!

PRAYER

*F*ather God, I continue to trust You for my every care. Lead me to trust You, to be still and know that You are God. Give me a peace that passes all understanding. Amen.

ACTION

*T*urn one of your struggles over to God. Let Him handle it for you. Write down the particulars in your journal, and be sure to date the entry. Check periodically to see how God is doing.

TODAY'S WISDOM

*D*on't worry about anything; instead, pray about everything; tell God your needs and don't forget to thank him for his answers. If you do this you will experience God's peace, which is far more wonderful than the human mind can understand. His peace will keep your thoughts and your hearts quiet and at rest as you trust in Christ Jesus.

PHILIPPIANS 4:6-7 TLB

Choose Life over Death

—⚬—

*I will lie down and sleep in peace, for you
alone, O LORD, make me dwell in safety.*
PSALM 4:8

$\mathcal{E}$ach day I must choose my attitude for the day. During times of pain and confusion, I must decide what I will be for the day. When I realize that God is my shield, my glory, and my hope, I can lift my head from a bowed position and serve the Lord, my God, today. He will give me joy for today.

We don't want to get into the trap of doing something just because it's the thing to do. We want to live a life that is meaningful to us and to our family. We want to make decisions according to these values, not according to what the media or random people whom we encounter tell us.

In order to live intuitively, we must have some quiet time to read and think. Hectic lives don't permit us to connect with the heartbeat of the soul. When we are too busy, we don't have time to dwell on the important issues of life. When we're rushed, we have an inner disturbance that prevents us from making well-thought-out decisions. When you and I are hurried in life, we have a tendency to have deep anger because we have relinquished the peace that comes from spending time with ourselves and the Lord. When our personal growth comes to a halt, it is because our spirit has not had times of stillness. Slow down.

PRAYER

God, let me be in tune with the feelings of my heart. Let me appreciate this alone time and come to know You and to know who I am. Amen.

ACTION

Slow down (and reap the rewards).

TODAY'S WISDOM

I have set before you life and death, the blessing and the curse. So choose life in order that you may live, you and your descendants.

DEUTERONOMY 30:19

What Posture for Prayer?

O Lord, hear me praying; listen to
my plea, O God my King, for I will never pray
to anyone but you.

PSALM 5:1 TLB

$\mathcal{D}$oes it make any difference to God in what position or setting we pray? Do we always have to kneel with our eyes closed and our hands clasped in order to come before the Lord? Is it proper to pray while driving to work in my car? Can I pray while cooking dinner? Must I have a prayer closet before God hears my words? What does Scripture have to say about proper posture for prayer?

In searching for the answer in the Word of God, I have discovered that all positions and all settings are proper and appropriate for prayer. God gives great liberty to praying people. The important factor is that our hearts are in communion with Him as we pray.

The following are some verses about how or when to pray:

- kneeling (1 Kings 8:54; Ezra 9:5; Daniel 6:10; Acts 20:36)
- standing (Jeremiah 18:20)
- sitting (2 Samuel 7:18)
- in bed (Psalm 63:6)
- in private (Matthew 6:6; Mark 1:35)

- with others (Psalm 35:18)
- hands lifted (1 Timothy 2:8)
- silently (1 Samuel 1:13)
- aloud (Acts 16:25).
- at all times (Luke 18:1)

The psalmist knows that God saves those who take refuge in Him. He assures God that He is the only One to whom he prays. Many times over the past few years I have come to God on my knees by my bed and cried out for Him to protect and heal me. As a child of God, I want to cuddle up to Him and feel His warmth and acceptance. I need His protection and assurance that I am His child and He hears my prayers.

PRAYER

*F*ather God, I know You don't care what position I'm in when I pray. Your concern is that I pray. May You hear my every prayer. Amen.

ACTION

*D*uring the next week, try several different positions as you pray.

TODAY'S WISDOM

*F*aith is not just about believing in God. It's about believing He'll do what He says—that He'll keep every promise He's made in the Holy Bible. When we are faithful, like God, we keep the promises we make. And when we have faith in another person, we believe they will keep the promises they have made.

ELAINE CREASMAN

God Has Big Ears

In the morning, O LORD, You will hear my
voice; in the morning I will order my prayer to
You and eagerly watch.

PSALM 5:3

*A*s I wake each new morning, I can be assured that my heavenly Father will be the same this day as the one before. Even though people might fail me, He will never let me down. I am confident when I approach His throne that I will be in His presence. I am never left out. When I pray to Him, He listens intently and attentively, with the care of a loving Father.

God has a past record of hearing all of my prayers and answering them. He hasn't always responded to them as quickly as I might have liked, and His answers were not always the ones I wanted to hear, but He has never failed to give me what I needed and more. I need to remember this truth on those mornings (and evenings) when God seems far away. No matter how I feel, He's listening.

I often have women ask me, "When should I pray?" The psalmist suggests that we pray in the morning. Let God hear your voice and petitions at the beginning of the day. I certainly don't pray only in the morning. I find myself offering utterances throughout my day and even into the darkest hours. I begin the day with thanksgiving, and I close the day with thanksgiving.

Notice also the psalm writer says that he waits and watches

eagerly. Eagerly for what? Answers to his requests in his morning prayers. Do you pray with the confidence that God hears your voice as you utter your praise, thanksgiving, confessions, and petitions? If we utter them, God hears them. He even hears them when we are not able to speak.

Frederick W. Robertson says, "Pray till prayer makes you forget your own wish, and leave it or merge it into God's will."

PRAYER

*F*ather God, I love to start my day off in prayer. It gets me off to a good start. I'm ready for the day and all that comes my way. Amen.

ACTION

*P*ray with eager expectations.

TODAY'S WISDOM

*C*hrist with me, Christ before me, Christ behind me, Christ in me, Christ beneath me, Christ above me, Christ on my right, Christ on my left, Christ when I lie down, Christ when I sit down, Christ when I arise, Christ in the heart of every man who thinks of me, Christ in the mouth of everyone who speaks of me, Christ in every eye that sees me, Christ in every ear that hears me.

ST. PATRICK

The Eyes of the Lord
Are upon Me

*Be gracious to me, O LORD, for I am
pining away; heal me, O LORD, for
my bones are dismayed.*

PSALM 6:2

*I*n this psalm, David is asking God how long the punishment, the suffering will last. He cries out, "Pity me, O Lord, for I am weak; heal me, for my body is sick." I know a little of the feelings behind David's petition because I had the same utterances in my life when my doctor announced that I had cancer. Little did I realize how sick I was to become or how long the road ahead of me would be. There were moments when I didn't think there would be another day in my life. Because of the chemo and radiation and all the medication I was taking, I could not keep my food down. I had to be careful not to get an infection, my body ached, my face was swollen, and my energy level was at zero.

My Bob and I bombarded God several times a day, asking Him to deliver me from this prison of illness. At times it didn't seem like He was even listening to our pleas. Often we were discouraged, but we hung our faith onto the character of God and all of His promises. After about four years of prayers and treatment, we could see the evidence of God's answers.

Little did I realize that someday I would have the quality of life that I presently experience. Where once I lay helpless on a bed, I now am experiencing about 90 percent of my previous level of good health.

God acts beyond our ability to understand, and thank goodness for that. Only by the grace of God am I able to speak and write as before. God is good! Are you waiting upon the Lord for an answer, for reprieve, for help? He has heard your cries and is answering them.

PRAYER

Lord, You are a God who keeps His promises. Your grace and will have restored me and turned my brokenness into wholeness. I praise You for each new day. Amen.

ACTION

Lay all your aches and pains at the cross.

TODAY'S WISDOM

After reading my book *Fill My Cup, Lord*, a young man wrote me and stated that he had written a song for me because he was so touched by the situation I had experienced. It was such an uplifting song for my own spirit that I wanted to share it with you.

The eyes of the Lord are upon me
For I love Him
He will take care of my each and every need
I'll be encouraged through hardship
I'll revere Him

I have all that I desire
For you see
The eyes of the Lord
Are forever upon me.
Lord, You are my hope
When my spirit's weak
I know You're with the brokenhearted
Those who will believe
I will trust You
You encourage me
I have no fear of what's ahead of me
The eyes of the Lord are forever upon me.

GLENN BAXLEY

Honor Your Name

—◆—

And those who know Your name
will put their trust in You.
PSALM 9:10 NKJV

It has been said, "All we own is our name." We are known by our name. Historically men took great effort in keeping a good reputation, because they wanted to protect the honor of their name. When people hear our name, what do they think of? Are we to be trusted, can we do what we say we will, will a friend loan us money knowing we will pay him back? Can someone confide in us and know we will be discreet? If a friend comes to us in trouble, do we offer God's wisdom and a prayerful heart?

Throughout the world, there is mighty power in the name of Jesus. Whenever His name is mentioned, it brings an audience to a pause. For us believers, it is a worthy name—one to be honored, one to be praised, one to be trusted. May our lives do nothing that would bring dishonor to this majestic name.

Wherever we go, we are a witness for that name. People will know Jesus by observing our lives. Either they will react favorably or they will shun His name. May our good deeds shine a bright light into a dark world. Will people think favorably on the name of Jesus because of us, or will they turn away from Him? We are accountable to Him for preserving His honor and good name.

PRAYER

*F*ather God, may Your name be honored by our lives. Let me realize that my actions will be seen by those around me. I want never to give Your name a bad reputation. I always want Your good name to be lifted up. Amen.

ACTION

*G*ive your children every reason to be proud of their family name.

TODAY'S WISDOM

Your Name

You got it from your father, 'twas the best he had to give.
And right gladly he bestowed it, it's yours the while you live.
You may lose the watch he gave you and another you may claim,
But remember, when you're tempted, to be careful of his name.

It was fair the day you got it, and a worthy name to bear,
When he took it from his father, there was no dishonor there.
Through the years he proudly wore it, to his father he was true,
And that name was clean and spotless when he passed it on to you.

Oh, there's much that he has given that he valued not at all.
He has watched you break your playthings in the days when you were small.
You have lost the knife he gave you, and you've scattered many a game,
But you'll never hurt your father if you're careful with his name.

It's yours to wear forever, yours to wear the while you live,
Yours perhaps, some distant morning, another boy to give.
And you'll smile as did your father—with a smile that all can share,
If a clean name and a good name you are giving him to wear.

EDGAR GUEST

Who May Dwell in Your Sanctuary?

LORD, who may dwell in your sanctuary? Who may live on your holy hill? He whose walk is blameless and who does what is righteous, who speaks the truth from his heart and has no slander on his tongue, who does his neighbor no wrong and casts no slur on his fellowman, who despises a vile man but honors those who fear the LORD, who keeps his oath even when it hurts, who lends his money without usury and does not accept a bribe against the innocent. He who does these things will never be shaken.

PSALM 15:1-5

In order to reside in God's sanctuary, He has some very tough requirements of character. How many times have we watched sport stars, politicians, business influencers, and even church leaders fall from societal favor because of wrongdoing? Think how fast we can fall away from God's even higher standards. We search for integrity, but it is difficult to find in our culture, in our world. It must become our desire to be worthy of God's sanctuary. Our character must be strong, and our willingness to follow His ways even stronger.

Though this psalm is written in the masculine gender, it has parallel implications for the female gender. As the Proverbs 31 lady ventured out beyond her homemaking skills, we find that many of our women today also go beyond the responsibilities of the home. Many of us have job responsibilities that take us into the world of business. We, like men, must exhibit virtue, integrity, honesty, and valor. David describes the character of the person (male and female) who qualifies to be a guest of God's sanctuary. These qualities, which are not natural, are imparted by God and by His Holy Spirit.

Let's see what we can glean from this great psalm regarding who will qualify to enter God's sanctuary:

- He/she walks blamelessly.
- He/she does what is righteous.
- He/she speaks the truth from his/her heart.
- He/she has no slander on his/her tongue.
- He/she does his/her neighbor no harm.
- He/she casts no slur on his/her fellowman.
- He/she despises an evil person.
- He/she honors those who fear the Lord.
- He/she keeps his/her oath even when it hurts.
- He/she loans his/her money without usury.
- He/she does not accept a bribe against the innocent.

Wow! These certainly are honorable characteristics! We certainly can appreciate the virtue of this type of person. Many times we look upon the life of a righteous person and say to ourselves, "It must be easy for him/her to be a Christian. He/she must not have the struggles with sin like I do!" Yet anyone who is trying to live a good and righteous life knows that we all must choose to serve our Lord each and every day. It isn't easier for any of us. We must decide to do what is right moment by moment.

David closes this psalm by stating, "He who does these things will never be shaken." What a great promise! One thing I do know:

If we live righteously, we sleep better at night. Now let's live with great faith.

PRAYER

*F*ather God, may I choose to live righteously every day. I know it isn't easy, but it can be done. I willfully decide today to believe and live the faith as the saints of old. Amen.

ACTION

*T*hink on the 11 characteristics of an honorable man/woman.

TODAY'S WISDOM

*H*old yourself responsible for a higher standard than anyone else expects of you. Never excuse yourself.

HENRY WARD BEECHER

Leaving a Beautiful Heritage

The lines have fallen to me in pleasant places;
indeed, my heritage is beautiful to me.

PSALM 16:6

$\mathscr{A}$ few years ago we had the pleasure to be in Abilene, Texas, to give an organizational seminar for a local church. We took an extra day to drive to Bob's birthplace in the small nearby town of Hawley, and then we continued on to his grandfather's homestead farm in Anson. We drove out to the farm for the first time in 55 years. As we drew near, I could see countless memories flash before Bob's eyes. He quickly went back in time to share the vivid memories of the past. The home and barn had long been torn down, but he escorted me to the site of the home, the outdoor cellar, the barn, the corrals, and the pastures where the horses roamed.

For the first time, I was able to actually see what Bob had been sharing with me verbally over these many years. We took pictures to recapture the fondness of the past, and Bob even brought home an old brick from the foundation of the farmhouse.

In his book *Locking Arms,* Stu Weber states,

> Heritage matters. People need clear, steady tracks to follow.
> It's by divine design....Not so very long ago, God himself
> left clear human footprints in the dust of our little world,
> tracks infinitely more indelible than those left by Apollo

31

astronauts on the airless moon. Memory is the great encourager of spirit and life, of connectedness. And rehearsing the past is a sacred practice. It sets the present course. It gives perspective.

In this age, when families move and roots aren't able to go deep, we need to take the time to share with our family the elements of our inheritance. What and who has gone before us is very important to who we are today. Our grandchildren love to sit in our laps and go through picture albums that have been maintained over the years. Each of our grandchildren has his or her own albums with images from the day Mom went to the hospital pregnant and came home with a precious child of God.

Are you building a delightful inheritance for your children? Will they look back and say they had rich experiences growing up? Do they know who they are? Can they recognize the pillars of your families? When your time comes to be with God in heaven, will you have left strong, deep tracks for those who follow? If not, start today. Begin to live with a purpose.

PRAYER

*F*ather God, thank You for giving me a delightful inheritance—one that has been easy to follow, because the tracks made by those who came before me are so clear and lead me in the right direction. Amen.

ACTION

*T*his evening around the dinner table have each member of the family share something that sticks out in his or her mind.

TODAY'S WISDOM

*A*s David concludes in Psalm 16:11: "You will make known to me the path of life; in Your presence is fullness of joy; in Your right hand there are pleasures forever."

Longer Than Twelve Inches

—◦—

I have set the LORD continually
before me; because He is at my right hand,
I will not be shaken.

PSALM 16:8

A wooden ruler is a remarkable aid in measuring distance. I use the ruler to help me while I'm measuring fabric for a new apron, a piece of wood to repair a damaged section of molding, or a length of ribbon to wrap a gift. We know that 12 inches equals a foot, but what is the significance of 18 inches?

Did you know that at any moment of your life, you're only 18 inches away from the hope you need? It's absolutely true. But those 18 inches may be the longest distance you will ever travel. That's the approximate distance from the top of your head to your heart. That's the critical distance you have to travel in order to live with an enduring, unquenchable hope.

You can't live in your head and live in hope. Enduring hope has to reside in your heart—the seat of all your emotions, your will, your connection with meaning. Hope comes when you invite the God who made you, the Christ who redeemed you, the Spirit who surrounds you—the triune God—to travel the same 18-inch journey from your head to your heart.

How do you make the trip? You have to take a leap of faith, which is not easy. You have to weigh the evidence: the testimony of the Bible; the life experiences of other people; and the still, small voice in your heart that keeps encouraging you to accept Jesus as your Savior. You've simply got to take a deep breath and make that "small," bottomless jump. Once you've done it, your hope for your life increases dramatically.

There are times when you can't let your mind overrule your heart. Make sure today that there is a consistency between mind and heart. It is such a short distance between these two nerve centers, but probably the most important 18 inches you will ever measure.[1]

PRAYER

*F*ather God, thank You for accompanying me on that journey from head to heart. I thank You for my salvation. Amen.

ACTION

*I*f you haven't taken that 18-inch journey, do so today.

TODAY'S WISDOM

A highly esteemed young man was rescued from the salty water, and he appeared to be dead. At length, he began to show signs of life. A thrill of joy ran through the crowd as it was whispered around, "He breathes!" How much greater the joy of men and angels over newly born souls!

Be a Woman of Joy

*You will make known to me the path of life;
in Your presence is fullness of joy; in Your right
hand there are pleasures forever.*

PSALM 16:11

*W*hen we have joy, we exhibit a celebration that is much larger than everyday happiness. We are filled with joy when we realize that we are loved by God. When we have the joy of the Lord, we can honestly be joyful for a new day, a new sunset, a new baby, a new season, a starting over. We are able to rejoice when we have the joy of the Lord in our heart.

Someone once asked Mother Teresa what the job description was for anyone who might wish to work alongside her in the dirty streets of India, with the stench of human waste and the overflowing of death in the densely populated city of Calcutta. Without a second thought, she responded, "The desire to work hard and a joyful attitude."

What great advice for all of us, regardless of where we live or what we do. If we are willing to work hard and exhibit a joyful attitude, we will be successful in life. It's no fun to be around those who are lazy and exhibit little or no joy. I have also noticed that people who have a lot of friends are those who work hard and are able to do so with joy. I want to learn these valuable traits from successful people. When I feel down, I want to exhibit joyfulness, and when I feel lazy, I want a new zeal in my body.

Frank C. Laubach stated it very nicely when he wrote, "Your joy comes from what you give, not from what you accumulate." The richest person leaves everything when she dies. Only her joy will be a living legacy for those who are left behind.

PRAYER

*F*ather God, I want to live a life beyond happiness; I want to experience and express Your joy. My heart yearns to be full of joy, reflecting Your participation in my life. Amen.

ACTION

*B*e known as a woman who expresses joy.

TODAY'S WISDOM

*A*ll sorts of things can undermine happiness—time, change, and tragedy above all. There isn't anything intrinsically wrong with happiness, but waiting for just the right circumstances or the ideal situation in order to be happy will keep you from fully living your life and experiencing God's joy.

But the answer is not to reject happiness, it is to go beyond it, to joy….Rooted in God, empowered by the energies of the resurrection, joy does not depend on getting the right income, the perfect spouse, the right mix of things. Joy goes so far beyond happiness that it is present even in the midst of deep unhappiness.

REBECCA M. PIPPERT

The Lord Is

The Lord is...

PSALM 23:1

$\mathcal{A}$t the beginning of Psalm 23, David's most beautiful psalm of trust, we read, "The Lord is..." That's all we need to know. "The Lord is." He is all we need. We don't need any other. He is the center of our life. All else revolves around Him. He is what makes sense out of the nonsense of this crazy world.

When my good health was disrupted by cancer, I started each new day with this proclamation: The Lord *is*...

- my supporter
- my courage
- my encourager
- my trust
- my salvation
- my purpose

He is my beginning and the end and all that falls between. Nothing else matters but Jesus. He is the Rock of my foundation. He is the Hearer and Responder to my prayers. At times I haven't even known how to pray, but I know that the Holy Spirit intercedes for me.

David pictures the Lord as the great Shepherd who provides

for and protects His sheep. How do you see the Lord? Have you called out to Him as your shepherd, courage, salvation, or provider? Everything that I have, everything that I am, is credited to Him who has made me. My whole purpose in life only matters as it revolves around my relationship with my Lord.

The Lord is everything. He is everything for me and for you.

PRAYER

*F*ather God, may I never forget to call on You in every situation. Thank You for being within the sound of my voice. You are all to me. Amen.

ACTION

*C*omplete: The Lord is _____.

TODAY'S WISDOM

*I*f I can stop one heart from breaking,
I shall not live in vain;
If I can ease one life the aching,
Or cool one pain,
Or help one fainting robin
Unto his nest again,
I shall not live in vain.

EMILY DICKINSON

The Lord Is My Shepherd

*Even though I walk through the valley of the
shadow of death, I fear no evil; for You are with
me; Your rod and Your staff, they comfort me.*

PSALM 23:4

*I*t was a cool February evening in California. My 88-year-old Jewish auntie's hospital room had its lights dimmed to gray. It had been a few days since I had seen her. We had such a nice visit then. She was alert as we talked about family and how she missed Uncle Hy, who had passed away nine months earlier. Now she lay there so thin and frail. Her breathing was heavy and irregular.

As I sat by her bedside holding her cool, clammy hand, I thought of the other times I had seen her in similar situations. Auntie had a surgery 25 years earlier and, because of complications, she almost died. A few years later, she was a passenger in a car that rolled down a steep hill and hit a power pole. Again she almost died. As life went on, illnesses came and went, but mostly came. The doctors had told us three times in the past year that Auntie wouldn't make it through the night. But she always did. Was this February night going to be any different? The doctor had been in to check on her and just shook his head. The rabbi arrived for a visit, but there was no response from Auntie. Would this be the night she would give up her fight for life?

On the other side of the curtain that was partially drawn in the shared hospital room was a charming, late-middle-aged Jamaican woman who was almost blind and suffered from diabetes. She spoke eight languages and had a sweet sense of peace and joy in spite of her pain. We enjoyed talking with her and found out that she was a Christian believer who grew up learning to read from the Bible. Every night before she closed her eyes to sleep, she would recite Psalm 23. On sleepless nights, she would repeat it over and over again. As she talked, I felt our spirits meet. In only a few hours with her I knew I loved that woman.

On this evening, Auntie's breathing was very labored. I leaned over to pat her forehead and give her a last hug good-bye. My lips were by her ear when the Spirit of God began to speak from my lips: "The Lord is my Shepherd, I shall not want." Then the angel from "bed B" joined me: "He makes me lie down in green pastures." It was like the sound of a million voices surrounding the room. "Even though I walk through the valley of the shadow of death, I will fear no evil, for you are with me; your rod and your staff, they comfort me." That precious woman and I ended the psalm as a duet. "You prepare a table before me in the presence of my enemies. You anoint my head with oil; my cup overflows. Surely goodness and love will follow me all the days of my life, and I will dwell in the house of the Lord forever."

With a last kiss, Bob and I walked out of the hospital room forever. Thirty minutes later Auntie died, with the words of the Twenty-third Psalm surrounding her room.[2]

PRAYER

*F*ather God, this psalm has been such a comfort for me over the years. Truly You have given me a peace in the past, You are giving me a peace in the present, and I am confident You will give me peace in the future. Amen.

ACTION

*M*emorize the complete Twenty-third Psalm.

TODAY'S WISDOM

*O*ur life is like a garden,
and with God's love and care
it blossoms with the flowers
of His blessings everywhere.

JOHN PAUL MOORE

Dwelling in the House of the Lord

—◦⦿◦—

Surely goodness and lovingkindness will
follow me all the days of my life, and I will
dwell in the house of the LORD forever.
PSALM 23:6

*W*ouldn't it be wonderful to know that we are already registered to be a guest in the house of the Lord forever? It will be better than any six-star hotel with beach and golf privileges. It will be beyond our imagination.

What a great truth to know that God actually loves and cares for us! As a young girl, I had a difficult time realizing that God died on the cross just for me. Somehow I felt that I had to pay for my salvation—and if not pay, at least work hard for it. But everything, including my final dwelling place, is free.

Jesus must have a lot of patience to wait for us to come to that conclusion. I'm sure He longs and cries for our repentance, but we just go along living our own selfish lives, doing our own thing—whatever that thing might be.

Campus Crusade provides a very simple little booklet which outlines four principles that will help you know God personally and experience the abundant life He promised in John 10:10:

1. God loves you and created you to know Him personally (John 3:16; John 17:3).

2. Man is sinful and separated from God, so we cannot know Him personally or experience His love (Romans 3:23; 6:23).

3. Jesus Christ is God's only provision for man's sin. Through Him alone we can know God personally and experience His love (Romans 5:8; 1 Corinthians 15:3-6; John 14:6).

4. We must individually receive Jesus Christ as Savior and Lord; then we can know God personally and experience His love (John 1:12; Ephesians 2:8-9; John 3:1-8; Revelation 3:20).[3]

PRAYER

*F*ather God, I want to know You personally. Thank You for dying on the cross for my sins. I open the door of my life and receive You as my Savior and Lord. Thank You for forgiving my sins and giving me eternal life. Take control of the throne of my life. Make me the kind of person You want me to be. Amen.

ACTION

*P*lace this date on the first page of your Bible. Contact a friend and let that person know of your decision.

TODAY'S WISDOM

*D*ear Friend,

I just had to send a note to tell you how much I love you and care about you. I saw you yesterday as you were walking with your friends. I waited all day hoping you would want to talk with me also. As evening drew near, I gave you a sunset to close your day and a cool breeze to rest you. And

I waited. But you never came. It hurt me, but I still love you because I am your friend.

I saw you fall asleep last night, and I longed to touch your brow. So I spilled moonlight on your pillow and your face. Again I waited, wanting to rush down so we could talk. I have so many gifts for you. But you awakened late the next day and rushed back to work. My tears were in the rain.

Today you looked so sad, so all alone. It makes my heart ache because I understand. My friends let me down and hurt me so many times, too. But I love you. Oh, if you would only listen to me. I really love you. I try to tell you in the blue sky and in the quiet green grass. I whisper it in the leaves on the trees and breathe it in the colors of the flowers. I shout it to you in the mountain streams and give the birds love songs to sing. I clothe you with warm sunshine and perfume the air with nature's scents. My love for you is deeper than the oceans and bigger than the biggest want or need in your heart.

If you only knew how much I want to help you. I want you to meet my Father. He wants to help you, too. My Father is that way, you know. Just call me, ask me, talk with me. I have so much to share with you. Yet I won't hassle you. I'll wait because I love you.

Your Friend,
Jesus

AUTHOR UNKNOWN

Lift a Prayer Heavenward

To You, O LORD, I lift up my soul.
O my God, in You I trust.

PSALM 25:1

Lifting up our soul to the Lord in prayer is one of the great expressions of our faith. Prayer can seem such a mystery. When do we pray, how do we pray, what do we say, what language do we speak? What exactly is prayer? We might answer that prayer is asking God for things, but surely it's more than that.

Some people think prayer is only for emergencies. Danger threatens, sicknesses come, things are lacking, difficulties arise, then they pray like the atheist in a coal mine. When the roof began to fall, he began to pray. There are many stories of soldiers who had no faith going into battle, but while in battle they began to utter prayers.

Prayer reminds us that we are utterly dependent upon God. We draw closer to God and become more knowledgeable about Him when we talk to Him. The more we discover about God, the richer our lives become.

Biblical dictionaries define *prayer* as "a wish directed toward God." When we pray, we are talking to God. It is really lifting our souls to God. When we do this, God has an opportunity to do what He wills in us and with us and through us. We make ourselves available to Him. An old Jewish saying puts it wonderfully: "Prayer is the moment when heaven and earth kiss each other." Prayer certainly is not our attempt to persuade God to do our will; however, it may release His power. In Matthew 6:10 it states, "Your will be done." After all, this is why we pray—to have God's will revealed in our lives and for us to experience that revelation.

PRAYER

*F*ather God, share with me the mystery of prayer. At times I get confused about prayer, but I don't want my prayers to request anything that isn't good for me. I truly want Your will to be done in my life. Amen.

ACTION

*L*ift up your soul in prayer today.

TODAY'S WISDOM

*A*nswers to prayer often come in unexpected ways. We pray, for instance, for a certain virtue; but God seldom delivers Christian virtues all wrapped in a package and ready for use. Rather he puts us in situations where by his help we can develop those virtues. Henry Ward Beecher told of a woman who prayed for patience, and God sent her a poor cook. The best answers to prayer may be the vision and strength to meet a circumstance or to assume a responsibility.

C.R. FINDLEY

Search Me, O God

———

Cross-examine me, O Lord, and see
that this is so; test my motives and affections
too. For I have taken your lovingkindness
and your truth as my ideals.

PSALM 26:2-3 TLB

I have learned that God has a master plan for my life. There's great comfort in knowing it is His timetable I live by. I have already experienced so many of His seasons, and each one has been good in its own way.

One of the great accomplishments of life is learning to find rest in our appointed time and relishing the joys and challenges that come with each new stage of living: the excitement and possibilities of youth, the satisfaction and fulfillment of maturity, the wisdom and patience of later years.

Yes, I prayed to learn patience, but did God have to take me so literally? Was it really necessary for me to go through all the pain, blood transfusions, CAT scans, and other inconveniences that go with cancer treatment? I was ready for some little pop quizzes; I didn't really want the final exam. Aren't there supposed to be midterms along the way? Don't they have dress rehearsals before opening on Broadway?

This illness has been the hardest test of my life. At times I have wondered if I'm up to it. Yet even in the midst of all the difficulties,

I can see a little of what God is doing in my life. For one thing, this ordeal has forced me to examine my inmost heart—what I truly believe, what I am about, what my priorities are, and what I want to stand for. My motives and affections have withstood the examination! During my time of testing, I have confirmed that God's ideals really are my ideals, and that I want to walk in faithfulness to Him. Now if I could only get patience a little faster....

PRAYER

*F*ather God, I appreciate Your cross-examination of who I am. Each of us needs to have the spotlight on our life to expose those areas that need work. My recent illness has given me great opportunity to really see who I am. Amen.

ACTION

*D*on't be afraid of God's cross-examination. Consider how God is cross-examining you in your life right now. How has He in the past? What have you learned about your faith and character during these times? Write these lessons down.

TODAY'S WISDOM

*W*hen the sun is refusing to shine on your day
and you're finding it hard just to cope,
When you're seeing more rain clouds than stars in the sky
and you just feel like giving up hope,
That's the time when someone comes along with a smile
and a warm hug that says "It's okay—
Tomorrow is coming, so don't give up now—
brighter moments are soon on their way!"

EMILY MATTHEWS, FROM THE POEM "JUST A LITTLE HUG"

Promises for Believers

*I shall wash my hands in innocence, and I will
go about Your altar, O LORD.*
PSALM 26:6

*O*n occasion people can read a promise from Scripture and think
that it is written just for them, not understanding that promises are
only written for believers and not for unbelievers. The only excep-
tion would be prayers for forgiveness of sin and to claim salvation
for their own lives.

If unbelievers or even disobedient children of God had the
promise put into their hands that reads, "Whatsoever ye shall ask
in prayer, believing, ye shall receive," they would be sure to ask
for things that would support them in their unbelief or disobedience. But as is the person, such will be his prayers. God does not
honor the requests of people asking for things that would support
or encourage their own waywardness.

It is true that if we keep His commandments, He will answer our
prayer according to His will for our lives. If we reject God, He will
not answer our prayers until we repent. Leviticus 26:21,24 reads,
"If ye walk contrary unto me…then will I also walk contrary unto
you." KJV We will never have perfect innocence, but we can have
an innocence based on not wanting to rebel against God. We need
to approach God with honesty and reverence.

Praying with a heart of obedience and with a spirit of submission blesses our lives with the joy of walking with God and in His will. It is so amazing to lift up petitions and desires and know that they are heard, know that we will not be rejected because of our unbelief, and know we are safe in the grip of God's will for our life.

PRAYER

*F*ather God, may I always find favor from walking in Your will for my life. Continually reveal sin in my life so that I may never come to Your throne with a heart of disobedience. Amen.

ACTION

*C*onfess any known sin in your life to the Trinity.

TODAY'S WISDOM

*T*each the wise, and they will be wiser. Teach the righteous, and they will learn more. Fear of the LORD is the beginning of wisdom. Knowledge of the Holy One results in understanding. Wisdom will multiply your days and add years to your life. If you become wise, you will be the one to benefit. If you scorn wisdom, you will be the one to suffer.

PROVERBS 9:9-12 NLT

Shortcuts to Sanity

—◦—

For in the day of trouble He will conceal me in
His tabernacle; in the secret place of His tent
He will hide me; He will lift me up on a rock.
PSALM 27:5

*G*od is always providing a tabernacle, a tent, a shelter for us when we are in the time of need. I can certainly give testimony to this promise. Whenever I cry out for help, He seems to always be there with the cover and protection of His shelter. When I have disorganization, He gives me sanity. The Creator of the universe gives us the ultimate example of making time for refuge, for rest, for stillness. When creating the world, He took disorder and in six days created the whole universe. Then on the seventh day He modeled for us a day of rest.

The Book of Ecclesiastes says, "There is a time for everything and a season for every activity under heaven" (NIV). Oh, that we would truly take that to heart and slowly but surely find the time and the season for every activity under heaven. Here are some ideas that can help put sanity back in life:

- Our bodies have a natural clock. Use your body clock to time activities to your energy level. Some people like the morning, and others are more productive in the evening.
- Holidays and special occasions are very predictable. Shop

once a year for birthday and holiday cards. Make a list of the names of people you will be selecting gifts for this year. When sales come along, take that list with you and be on the lookout for a special something for each person. Write the gift alongside the name and list where/when it was purchased for easier record-keeping.

- Keep a gift shelf in your home for emergencies. As you shop throughout the year, be on the lookout for items that could serve a multitude of purposes: housewarming, birthday, get well, or "thank you for your hospitality." Have a gift-wrap box or drawer. Remember, it doesn't have to be perfect. And don't overdo your advance spending. Keep your gift list handy to avoid duplications.

There's a time for everything and a season for every activity. Start today to find that season.

PRAYER

Lord, thanks for lifting me up and placing me on a rock. I feel so secure when You are holding me on such a firm foundation. Amen.

ACTION

Let God put you in His tabernacle for safekeeping.

TODAY'S WISDOM

Not what we give, but what we share—for the gift without the giver is bare; who gives himself with his alms feeds three—himself, his hungering neighbor and Me.

James Russell Lowell

Who You Are in God

Hear, O LORD, when I cry with my voice, and
be gracious to me and answer me. When You
said, "Seek my face," my heart said to You,
"Your face, O LORD, I shall seek."

PSALM 27:7-8

*T*oday I hear so many people say, "I've got to leave my marriage so I can find out who I am." One of the great gifts of Scripture is that it tells us who we are in God. When we understand this identity, we do not expect to find out who we are in our wealth, our material possessions, our physical appearance, or in our marriage. These things are not where we are supposed to discover our identity.

Read the complete twenty-seventh chapter of Psalms. In this great anthem of praise, David expresses his confidence in the Lord (verses 1-6), prays for continued victory (verses 7-12), and rejoices in his waiting on the Lord (verses 13-14).

It is said in Scripture that David was a man after God's own heart. Even as a sinner, he was considered a truly godly man. In this passage we can select words that answer four basic questions about God and His presence in our lives:

1. Who is God?
2. What does God do?
3. Who are we?
4. What do we do?

If we search Scripture and understand the various aspects of God's character, we will never have to leave home to find out who we are. We will already know who we are because we know and understand who God is. One goes with the other.

Who God Is

- He is our Lord.
- He is our salvation.
- He is good.
- He is our defense in life.
- He is light.
- He is a teacher.
- He is our Savior.
- He is beauty.

What God Does

- He defends us.
- He keeps us safe.
- He will hide us.
- He lifts us up.
- He protects us from false witness.
- He hears our voice.
- He receives us unconditionally.
- He is sovereign.
- He puts us above circumstances.

Who We Are

- We are worshipers.
- We seek God.

- We are insecure because we do not ask.
- We have enemies.
- We need leadership.
- We are impatient.
- We experience rejection.
- We are fearful.
- We are learners.
- We are God's children.
- We are servants of God.
- We are petitioners in prayer.

What We Do

- We trust the worthiness of God.
- We are confident.
- We pray, we seek, we ask.
- We meditate in His temple.
- We wait upon the Lord.
- We seek the Lord's face.
- We desire to be in the house of the Lord.
- We sing praises with joy.
- We ask of God our petitions (prayer).
- We take courage.[4]

PRAYER

*F*ather God, it's hard to realize what a magnificent being You are. We try the best we can, but our minds aren't big enough to comprehend Your wonders. Instill in me a desire to search Your Word and absorb it into my very being. Amen.

ACTION

Select one truth from each of the four sections and meditate upon it today.

TODAY'S WISDOM

For the mountains may be removed and the hills may shake, but My lovingkindness will not be removed from you, and My covenant of peace will not be shaken," says the LORD who has compassion on you.

ISAIAH 54:10

What Do You Say?

*Blessed be the LORD, because He has heard the
voice of my supplication.*

PSALM 28:6

*W*hen we are in distress, we quickly send our prayers skyward, asking God to answer all of our requests, our wishes. "Give me this. I want that. Don't give me this. Protect me from harm. Heal me from cancer. Watch over my sick child." On and on we petition God for all kinds of miracles, but do we ever take time to thank Him for His presence, for His answers to those requests? We teach our children to say "thank you" when they are very young, but we often forget to say the same "magic words" when God so graciously gives us something.

One of the greatest reasons to record your prayer requests is so that you can reflect back on the many reasons you have to praise the Lord and to thank Him. There will still be times when you are waiting for your answer or hoping for a different answer. But when you trust in God's plan and purpose for you, you can lift up your thanks no matter what, because you know He has you in the palm of His hand and cares deeply about you and your life.

We should be quick to show our appreciation because our heavenly Father is pleased when we thank Him. I know I was pleased as a mom when I would hear my children tell someone "thank you" without me having to remind them to do so.

When our Lord was on earth, He lifted His voice to His Father and expressed thanks for food (John 6:11), for the simplicity of the gospel (Matthew 11:25), and for answered prayer (John 11:41).

Two little words—*thank you*—are so precious to the ears of God. Practice them often!

PRAYER

*F*ather God, as a mother I love to hear "thank you," so I know You must also love to hear "thank You" from us when You so graciously hear and answer our supplications.

ACTION

*T*hank God today!

TODAY'S WISDOM

*I*n the end we shall find every promise of God perfectly fulfilled. Then why should we not let our hearts rest in peace about everything that happens? Nothing can happen that can break a single one of these precious promises. There is no promise of an easy passage, but there are promises for every day of the voyage. Each day let us take one promise for our own, live on it, test and prove it—and thank God for it.

AMY CARMICHAEL

Here I Am Alive

O LORD, my God, I cried to You for help,
and You healed me. O LORD, You have brought
up my soul from Sheol [God delivered him
from the brink of death].

PSALM 30:2-3

*W*hen my doctor announced to me that I had cancer, I felt like my life left my body. I figured that it was all over. It was only a matter of time, and I would be dead. All my hopes, dreams, and aspirations were no more. The husband, the family, the friends, the home all would soon be past tense. Life that I once so enjoyed was never to be again.

Immediately I went into treatment, and I became a prisoner to the medical profession for the next seven years. I went through 500 hours of chemo, 22 days of radiation, a bone-marrow transplant from a 23-year-old Canadian, four stays of 10 days each in the hospital, and on and on. I experienced emotional and physical highs, and to balance it off I had some equal lows. The roller coaster kept lifting me up and bringing me down.

Have you ever asked yourself the question, "What do I know for sure?" When I ask myself that probing question in terms of my battle with cancer, a couple of things come to mind.

One thing I know is that God is good. That battle cry has become one of our family's mottos: "God Is Good." I knew it before, but now I really know it. Even when circumstances seemed unbearable, the Lord's goodness kept shining through. In each ordeal, I felt the bedrock reality of God's goodness underneath me.

And I know that God heals. I know this not just because I've read it in the Bible or met other people who have been healed; I know this because He has worked a miracle of healing in my life. It came about a little differently than I expected and took a lot longer than I thought, but it was still a bona fide, praiseworthy, hallelujah-inspiring miracle.

God heals, and He brought up my soul from death, from the pit of despair, from Sheol. I believe this with all my heart. I have also come to believe healing is a process we can't always understand. Only God knows His ways. I'm not capable of understanding why God does what He does. Someday in heaven I will know.

PRAYER

*F*ather God, thank You for delivering me. By Your grace Your stripes healed my stripes, and by Your stripes I am saved. Amen.

ACTION

*P*ray, believing that God will restore your health and any other situation you are experiencing.

TODAY'S WISDOM

*O*ne of the most tragic things I know about human nature is that all of us tend to put off living. We are all dreaming of some magical rose garden over the horizon—instead of enjoying the roses that are blooming outside our window today.

DALE CARNEGIE

Have Shouts of Joy

*Weeping may last for the night, but a shout
of joy comes in the morning.*

PSALM 30:5

*G*od does not allow affliction and grief in His children for nothing. Times of affliction and strife breathe life into our understanding of His wisdom and love. You are never asked to endure more than you can bear with Christ's strength. Do not be discouraged when you suffer. He shall make your vineyard blossom and your field yield its fruit. You shall again come forth with those who rejoice, and once more shall the song of gladness be on your lips. Hope yet, for there is hope in all of life's perils. Trust still, for you may have confidence in your trials. "Thou hast turned for me my mourning into dancing" (Psalm 30:11 KJV).

In the Book of Job, we read of Satan tempting Job and afflicting him, "and the LORD turned the captivity of Job, when he prayed for his friends" (Job 42:10 KJV). Intercessory prayer was the sign of Job's returning greatness. It was the rainbow in the cloud, the dove bearing the olive branch, the voice of the turtle announcing the coming summer. When Job's soul began to expand itself in holy and loving prayer for his erring brethren, the heart of God showed itself to him by returning his prosperity and making him full. Use this time of despair to intercede for other people. Forget about your situation, because it's not about you. Reach out to others, and you will have shouts of joy in the morning.

PRAYER

*F*ather God, life is truly not about me; it reaches beyond my grief and pain. As I give unto others, You greatly give to me. Amen.

ACTION

*I*ntercede for those in need.

TODAY'S WISDOM

*Y*ou will find, as you look back upon your life, that the moments that stand out are the moments when you have done things for others.

HENRY DRUMMOND

Living with Peace

*The angel of the LORD encamps around those
who fear Him, and rescues them.*

PSALM 34:7

$\mathcal{H}$ave you noticed that the promises of Scripture have a condition or requirement attached to them? In this particular promise, the requirement is that a person must fear the Lord. David the psalmist doesn't say that everyone is going to be rescued by the Lord—only those who are obedient to God's commands. This is a jewel of a statement and a promise. I find it very comforting to know that God has appointed an angel to look after my well-being.

As a child, did you ever build a clubhouse or a fort? Did you ever cover a table with a blanket and crawl inside to a safe, cozy nest? I did, and it was such a secure feeling. That's what Psalm 34 reminds me of. The word *encamps* denotes making a camp or a fortress for protection. That's what the Lord has done for each of us. David was a man on the run, not knowing if he would live or die. Each day he begged God for mercy. He petitioned for safety and the snug feeling of protection. Truly the Lord has given each of us our own special angel who wraps loving arms around us and delivers us from all harm.

I make it my practice to stand on the promise that no matter what happens, all's well. God is keeping a close, protective watch on me. I continually feel His presence. He's always near. Even when

I feel I have moved away from Him, He will never forsake me. I am His child. During my darkest hours, I can be assured that He is overseeing my every situation. I see nonbelievers around me with lives driven by fear, who are unable to experience peace in their situation. Don't wait much longer in life if you are living in fear rather than in the peace of faith.

PRAYER

Father God, You are my protector. You keep me safe when I need a shelter. When You are standing next to me, I feel so secure. Thanks for being my rock and foundation for life. Amen.

ACTION

Be courageous enough to call out to God when you are in need of His protection.

TODAY'S WISDOM

When you get in a tight place and everything goes against you till it seems you could not hold on a minute longer, never give up then, for that is just the place and time that the tide will turn.

HARRIET BEECHER STOWE

Becoming a Wise Person

---

*Fear the LORD, you his saints, for those
who fear him lack nothing....Come, my
children, listen to me; I will teach
you the fear of the LORD.*

PSALM 34:9,11 NIV

*H*ow does a person get wisdom? This is a basic question that men have asked for centuries. In the Book of Proverbs, we find verse after verse which attempts to answer that basic question of life. Proverbs 1:7 gives an answer to that question when it states: "The fear of the LORD is the beginning of knowledge; fools despise wisdom and instruction." The motto of the wisdom teachers and the theme of Proverbs is that the fear of the Lord is the starting point and essence of wisdom. The phrase "fear of the Lord" means a reverence for God expressed in submission to His will.

Wisdom is not acquired by a secret prescribed formula but through a right relationship with God. We can dig into the depths and wonders of the Bible to discover the riches of God's wisdom for each and every one of us. Some verses of Scripture that will help us understand this wisdom are found in:

- Proverbs 9:9-12
- James, chapter 3
- Isaiah 11:2-5
- Jeremiah 9:23-24

- Proverbs, chapter 8
- James 1:5-8
- Proverbs 4:5-7
- Ecclesiastes 12:9-13
- Daniel 12:3
- James 3:13
- Ephesians 5:15-17

Wisdom calls us to use the knowledge we have to take a proper course of action. If we have knowledge and don't act upon that knowledge, it is the same as not knowing at all. Knowing Christ will give us a source of wisdom in all that we do.

PRAYER

*F*ather God, give us wisdom to guide our children in today's information age. Help us show them the importance and joys of direct interaction with You and with other people. Amen.

ACTION

*H*elp your children move beyond the gathering of information and teach them how to touch someone's life with God's love.

TODAY'S WISDOM

*T*heodore Roosevelt (1858–1919), the United States' twenty-sixth president, is quoted as saying, "Almost every man who has by his lifework added to the sum of human achievement of which the race is proud, of which our people are proud, almost every such man has based his lifework largely upon the teachings of the Bible."

Seek the Shadow of His Wings

How precious is Your lovingkindness,
O God! And the children of men take refuge in
the shadow of Your wings.

PSALM 36:7

As a young girl, I loved to look down at the sidewalk on a bright, sunny day and see the shadows of the clouds and planes as they flew overhead. Living in the warm southern California climate, I appreciated the big clouds because they blocked out the sun's hot rays and gave some relief from the noonday sun.

I can only imagine what kind of shadow God's wings would cast. I know it would be much larger than the shadow of a sparrow, even larger than that of an American bald eagle, or even a California condor. I can just feel the cool shade of His presence. I'm so glad I can relax in the shadow of His mighty wings and under the protection of His watchful eye.

My cancer journey has given me a wonderful opportunity to do things in a new and different way. I've been able to truly be still and know that He is God. I was so caught up in such a hectic pace that I didn't take the time to look up toward heaven and see His big, puffy clouds, or to look down and pay attention to the shadows on the sidewalk. Now I simply make the time.

As I wake each new morning, I can be assured that the shadow of His wings is around me. Even though people might fail me, He will never let me down. I am confident that when I approach His throne, I will be in His presence. When I pray to Him, He listens.

Zephaniah 3:5 (NIV) reassures me that "the Lord…is righteous; he does no wrong. Morning by morning he dispenses his justice, and every new day he does not fail."

PRAYER

*L*ord above all, Your protective shadow surrounds me every day. You give shade to comfort my soul, and You send a refreshing breeze my way when my cheeks are hot. I appreciate Your relief when the heat of life threatens to overpower me. Amen.

ACTION

*R*each skyward to seek the protection of God's wings.

TODAY'S WISDOM

*W*hen things go wrong, as they sometimes will,
When the road you're trudging seems all uphill,
When the funds are low and the debts are high,
And you want to smile but you have to sigh,
When care is pressing you down a bit,
Rest if you must, but don't you quit.

Life is strange with its twists and turns
As every one of us sometimes learns;
And many a failure turns about
When he might have won had he stuck it out.
Don't give up though the pace seems slow;
You may succeed with another blow!

Success is failure turned inside out,
The silver tint of the clouds of doubt;
And you never can tell just how close you are,
It may be near when it seems so far.
So stick to the fight when you're hardest hit;
When things seem worst, you must not quit.

AUTHOR UNKNOWN

Surviving Hard Situations

Do not fret because of evildoers.
PSALM 37:1

*H*ave you ever stayed up late, staring at the ceiling and worrying about the evil in the world, the wrongdoings, and the potential of harm coming to you or to your loved ones? It is very easy to become consumed by fear, by fretting. But God does not want us to fall into this cycle of despair. And we don't want to waste our days or our nights frozen with fear when there is so much life to be lived and embraced.

Our souls long for the peace and security that only God can provide. In Psalm 37, David offers us great advice and wisdom to ease our minds and hearts:

- Trust God (verse 3): Many times people will disappoint us, but God never will.
- Do good things (verse 3): The more good we do, the less chance that evil can make an impact.
- Delight in the Lord (verse 4): Take delight in the things of the Lord. He promises to meet our needs.
- Commit your way to God (verse 5): He will be a blessing to you.
- Wait patiently for the Lord (verse 7): He will overcome every situation.

The more time we spend studying God's Word and being around positive influences, the less time we have to worry. Martin Luther once said, "The more time we study the Word the more time we will pray and the more time we pray the more time we will study God's Word. When we start with one, we will finish with the other."

PRAYER

*F*ather God, I want to grow so close to You that I won't have time for the negatives of my life. I thank You for getting me through the hard situations of life. Amen.

ACTION

*T*ake all of your hard situations to the Lord.

TODAY'S WISDOM

*T*he way
each tiny flower
reaches up to heaven
with trust,
we, too, should lift
our hearts to God
and know He cares
for us.

AGNES SLIGH TURNBULL

Boldly Say No

*Rest in the LORD and wait patiently
for Him; do not fret because of him
who prospers in his way.*

PSALM 37:7

One of the Barnes' mottos is, "Say no to good things and save your yeses for the best." We all are living hurried lives, and we can get bogged down with a lot of commitments if we aren't careful. When we overcommit, our good attitudes can turn into frustration, our health begins to show signs of wear and tear, our emotions become fragile, we have no time to socialize and enjoy other relationships, and we drop the ball on our spiritual growth and development. In short, we become people who are not too fun to be around and who, in the end, are not serving anyone very effectively—including God.

Is business worth us falling apart? I don't think so. As I look around and see how healthy people cope, I find that the really healthy ones live a balanced life. Along the way they have boldly learned how to say no. One of my Bob's favorite expressions for our family is *moderation.* There is a time and place when we all have to realize that too much of any good thing becomes a weakness. Through moderation we can get back to a balanced life.

As I speak to many groups across America, I find numerous women who are just plain burned out. They are exhausted and have very little time for themselves. They say, "There is no time to stop and smell the roses. I've always got to be somewhere else and doing what other people want me to do. There is no time for me." It seems like there is no letting up. Everyone wants us to go faster and faster, to hurry, hurry. We've got to come to grips with our lives and take control. There are times when we have to boldly say no.

In order to prevent burnout or to renew ourselves after a burnout, we need to take care of four aspects of our lives:

1. Physical—exercise, manage stress in positive ways, sleep eight hours a night
2. Mental—read, think, plan, write
3. Spiritual—engage in Bible study, prayer, fellowship, service
4. Emotional/social—volunteer, get involved, be informed, connect

We must be proactive if we are going to grow in these four areas. No couch potatoes allowed. No one can do it for us or make it urgent for us. We must do it ourselves and for ourselves. Allow yourself times for renewal and reenergizing. Figure out what gives you refreshment, and bring your burdens to the Lord.

PRAYER

*F*ather God, oh, how I need to learn to wait upon You. Give me courage to say no. Amen.

ACTION

*S*tart renewal today! Choose a way to grow in one of the four main areas of life.

TODAY'S WISDOM

*S*uppose you came upon a man in the woods feverishly sawing down a tree.

"You look exhausted!" you exclaim. "How long have you been at it?"

"Over five hours," he replies, "and I'm beat. This is hard."

"Maybe you could take a break for a few minutes and sharpen that saw. Then the work would go faster."

"No time," the man says emphatically. "I'm too busy sawing."

STEPHEN R. COVEY

You Are Not Alone

Lord, all my desire is before You; and my
sighing is not hidden from You.

PSALM 38:9

*T*here is nothing lonelier than loneliness. Satan loves to move in during our darkest hour and take away all of our joy. He seems to wait until we are at our lowest point (usually at night) to whisper in our ear that God has forsaken us and He offers no hope. These dark hours are tests for us as believers. We are no longer talking about theories and philosophies of life. We are confronted with the reality of life. Do we really believe what we say we believe? Now is the time to walk our talk.

Sometimes during the night while I sleep I let out a sigh, and my Bob inquires if I am okay. I'm often unaware that a sigh has been uttered. I assure Bob that I am okay, and that my soul was just talking to God.

Perhaps my sigh is saying, "Lord, in my sickness and distress, my whole life is open before You. I've hidden nothing from You. You even hear my sighs. At times, my words don't seem adequate; all that are left are the groans of my soul. I look forward to what You will reveal next. Your plan is my plan."

As my journey is going in the direction of recovery, I thank God every day for how He is restoring my health to where it was. I am enjoying a quality of life that I never thought I would have. All that the locusts have eaten has been restored to me and my family. One of the big mysteries of life is why He has restored health to me and not to other people. He is the Potter of my life. I just have to trust Him in life and in death.

I do know that in sickness and in health we should allow our souls to speak to God often. Utter those sighs of fear, disappointment, weariness, and hope so that the Potter may turn your heartache into something new. The next time night falls and loneliness emerges, you will know that He is there to see you through to the dawn.

PRAYER

*F*ather God, the tears of my sighs have been evident on my pillow. I'm glad You have collected each and every one of them in Your bottle. Thank You for hearing my faintest sigh. Amen.

ACTION

*T*rust God and give your sighs to Him.

TODAY'S WISDOM

*G*od hath not promised skies always blue,
Flower-strewn pathways all our lives through;...
But God hath promised strength for the day,
Rest for the labor, light for the way,
Grace for the trials, help from above,
Unfailing sympathy, undying love.

ANNIE FLINT

Having Joy in Your Heart

He put a new song in my mouth, a
song of praise to our God.

PSALM 40:3

*W*hat would our life be without joy? We would be like a violin out of tune; it yields such harsh sounds. Life without joy is like a bone out of joint; it doesn't function properly, and it gives pain with each movement. We cannot do anything well without joy. Joy is what lubricates our whole life. It causes us to greet one another when the circumstances of life cause us to think, "I don't want to meet anyone today. Let me roll around in my own pity."

Lack of joy causes heartache within our own personal life, but it also overflows into the lives around us. What does it really mean to have joy in our life? Happiness and fun are good, but they come and go with circumstances. Joy, however, is felt beyond our circumstances. Joy can be experienced even when times are difficult.

Joy is an attitude we have toward life's experiences. It is a treasure of the heart, a comforting knowing of God's intimate presence. As we view the events of our life, we can choose to be resentful toward God for letting certain things happen to us, or we can choose an attitude of gratitude and a commitment to joy. Joy is by far the best choice.

We have joy when we are serving God and doing what He wants for our lives. We have joy when we learn to take our circumstances and the ups and downs of life in stride and use all situations to bring glory to God. We lighten our load in life and draw other people to us by having a joyful heart. When we have joy in the Lord, we begin to see life from God's point of view, and we realize that things have never looked so beautiful, so peaceful, so amazing. The joy of the Lord is our strength.

PRAYER

Father God, let my life reflect my joy in You. Your promises are what give me joy through all situations. If I looked at the events of my daily life, I would often have a frown, but just knowing You gives me great hope. Thank You for Your gift of joy. Amen.

ACTION

Be full of joy today. Reflect God's goodness to those around you.

TODAY'S WISDOM

Find joy in simplicity, self-respect, and indifference to what lies between virtue and vice. Love the human race. Follow the divine.

MARCUS AURELIUS

Start Each Day with Prayer

—⁂—

Thou, O LORD, will not withhold Your compas-
sion from me; Your lovingkindness and Your
truth will continually preserve me.

PSALM 40:11

*T*here is nothing like entering a new day and realizing that prayers of protection have been uttered for you this day. God has given me such wonderful friends, who surround me with prayers each day. They pray a prayer of protection for me that builds a hedge around my every event.

Our life journey takes us over many roads. Some are paved and don't have chuckholes; others have large potholes from lots of wear. Sometimes we travel over dirt roads that are dusty, and some roads even have been muddied by rain.

For me, my roads were beautifully paved until I was 58 years old, and then my road developed a lot of debris and divots. I always thought that my road was to be perfect, but my many travels in and through Cancerland put extra wear and tear on this perfectly designed path. When I heard that I had the big "C," I realized that this smooth journey had developed a fault line which I couldn't control or repair by my own endeavors. Fortunately, up to this point I had been in the Word, had a strong prayer life, and had confidence that God would be the Contractor to restore my roadway back to normal.

As you journey each day, ask God to grant you His mercy for

your emotional, physical, and spiritual travels and to protect you with His love and truth. We have no idea what lies before us, so we need the protection of God's presence, the power of prayer, and His preservation of our lives and spirits.

PRAYER

*F*ather God, in time all of our roads will deteriorate and will need to have repairs. Protect and preserve me as I start another day. Amen.

ACTION

*G*o to God in prayer for today's protection and provisions. See how you might be a part of God's care for another.

TODAY'S WISDOM

*W*hen the train goes through a tunnel and the world gets dark, do you jump out? Of course not. You sit still and trust the engineer to get you through.

CORRIE TEN BOOM

Let God Light Your Path

---

*Oh, send out your light and your truth—let
them lead me. Let them lead me to your Temple
on your holy mountain, Zion. There I will go
to the altar of God my exceeding joy, and praise
him with my harp. O God—my God!*

PSALM 43:3-4 TLB

I get upset with myself when I act so very human. I know what
I should do, but often I find that I lose sight of my Provider. My
spirit becomes gloomy, and I don't want that to be a part of my
present. I must continually trust in God.

Let Jesus' light and your present situation lead you to truth that
will put you in the presence of God. I have met countless people
who have found Jesus through their journey of pain or loss. I have
also witnessed a few who have rejected the truth. Most of this latter
group cut themselves off from their support groups and live in isolation and loneliness.

Even though I came into my personal difficult journey possessing
my Christian faith, I have experienced an abundance of growth in
my Christian walk. I have found that my altar to God is in my
prayer closet. I didn't spend time considering whether my coffee
or tea was weak or strong or had too much or too little cream. The
little things of life never appeared on the radar screen. I was able to
sing praises to God's name. This grander view of what is important

opened my eyes to the needs of other people and God's goodness in the midst of these needs.

PRAYER

*F*ather God, You light my path and give me wisdom to follow that path. You have made my life so exciting. Each day has new miracles, and I love the journey You have provided. Amen.

ACTION

*F*ollow the path God has been lighting for you.

TODAY'S WISDOM

What Is Faith?

Faith is the eye by which we look to Jesus.
A dim-sighted eye is still an eye; a weeping eye is still an eye.

Faith is the hand with which we lay hold of Jesus.
A trembling hand is still a hand. And he is a believer
Whose heart within him trembles when he touches the
Hem of the Savior's garment, that he may be healed.

Faith is the tongue by which we taste how good the
Lord is. A feverish tongue is nevertheless a tongue.
And then we may believe, when we are without
The smallest portion of comfort; for our faith is founded
Not upon feelings, but upon the promises of God.

Faith is the foot by which we go to Jesus. A lame foot
Is still a foot. He who comes slowly, nevertheless comes.

GEORGE MUELLER

A Big, Bright Smile

---

*Why are you in despair, O my soul? And why
are you disturbed within me? Hope in God, for
I shall again praise Him.*

PSALM 43:5

I have experienced the same dilemma that Paul had in Romans 7:15 and 19: "For what I am doing, I do not understand; for I am not practicing what I would like to do, but I am doing the very thing I hate....For the good that I want, I do not do; but I practice the very evil that I do not want." How about you? Have you ever felt a tug-of-war going on in your heart? You know what you want to do, what God calls you to do, but following through isn't easy.

That is the struggle of all mankind: the tension between good and evil. We know what we should do, but we find ourselves struggling to do it.

During hard times, this verse helped me to remember that He will make me smile again. Don't you just love to hear that assurance? When my spirit becomes gloomy, I can choose to continually trust in God. Christ does not force our will; He only receives what we give Him. We can either reject or receive His promises. I personally like gifts, particularly when they are free to the receiver.

Despite what's happening in our lives, we can say loud and clear, "I will not fear!" Time and time again, God has given me confidence that I can believe Him for the future. He is our refuge and strength.

The struggle will pass, and I will praise Him. I will smile again with confidence in His promises. Are you ready to smile?

PRAYER

Lord, thank You for letting me smile again. Your joy makes my heart praise You. May those around me see that my smile is from You. Amen.

ACTION

Smile a lot today! And let someone know why you smile.

TODAY'S WISDOM

Join the great company of those who make the barren places of life fruitful with kindness. Carry a vision of heaven in your hearts, and you shall make your name, your college, the world, correspond to that vision. Your success and happiness lie within you. External conditions are the accidents of life, its outer wrappings. The great, enduring realities are love and service. Joy is the holy fire that keeps our purpose warm and our intelligence aglow. Resolve to keep happy, and your joy and you shall form an invincible host against difficulty.

HELEN KELLER

His Plans Far Exceed Our Plans

My tongue is the pen of a ready writer.

PSALM 45:1

You have a story to tell. You might not realize it because you don't have an immediate reason to tell it or write it. But you have a story. Someday it may come out. I can remember back when I was a new empty nester; our two children were away at college, and my purpose in life had been fulfilled (at least I thought so). I got down on my knees beside my bed one morning and cried out to God to show me what I was to do for the rest of my life. I said, "God, if You can use me, I'm at Your service. I have no formal education. I have no working skills. I've been a homemaker for the last 18 years; that's all I know. Use me any way You can. I'm Yours."

At the same time, I had become acquainted with a prominent Christian writer and speaker by the name of Florence Littauer. After a couple years of friendship, she suggested that I might consider writing a book. I was dumbfounded. I didn't know how to write. Yes, I had spoken before large audiences about my Christian faith—with good response. But a writer? I had no confidence in that area.

Shortly after that conversation with Florence, I received a phone call from her publishing company and the president said, "I hear you have a book?" I said, "No, I don't have a book. I don't even know how to write one." After some time he asked me to send him any tapes, outlines, written materials pertaining to my area of expertise: home organization. I was glad to comply, but not very confident that anything would happen.

In about six weeks, I received in the mail a manuscript transcribed from my materials I had sent to the president. That book became my very first book, entitled *More Hours in My Day*. Twenty-two years and many revisions and reprints later, this book remains in print. That book was the beginning of a wonderful ministry that has brought God's words and principles to hundreds of thousands of readers. What I thought was insignificant, God knew would be built up to serve Him. Each day I am thankful for all those who encouraged me along the journey that has evolved into more than 65 titles and thousands of opportunities to speak to groups!

Each year I have the privilege to go to the Christian Booksellers Convention, which is now called the International Christian Retail Show. As I walk the huge convention floor, I literally see aisle after aisle of books written by various authors who have a story to tell.

A tongue devoted to God can accomplish much. God heard me when I asked for direction and the way to be used by Him. Use your tongue to tell people how God has impacted your life. Tell it through word of mouth or through the written word. God does great things with our prayers, with our desire to be used by Him, and with our stories. Place the unfolding story of your life in His hands and get ready to share it!

PRAYER

*F*ather God, I appreciate the confidence You have in me. Your vision for my life has been astounding. Thank You! Amen.

ACTION

*W*hat is your story? Begin to share it, write it, pray about it, and lift it up to God.

TODAY'S WISDOM

*O*ne truth about God which I continue to discover anew is that he has more for us than we can imagine. His plans far exceed our plans, and his grace makes possible so much more than we can envision.

NANCY PICKERING

Very Present Help

God is our refuge and strength,
a very present help in trouble.

PSALM 46:1

When a tragedy takes place, I say to myself, "How does someone go through these tough events of life without the sustaining power of the Trinity?" It just doesn't seem possible without the peace of God.

As I write these thoughts today, I am waiting to attend a funeral in four days for a young man killed in a dune buggy accident in a desolate desert location. He had everything that life could offer: youth, a wonderful family, material blessings, and his own very successful automobile agency. Thank God, he also trusted in the salvation of our Lord. But unexpected death challenges even believers' hearts. Fortunately we know that this young man is where he had planned as his final destination: heaven. We are saddened, but we do take great comfort in this fact.

One of the stories that helps me is about Horatio Spafford—a man who kept faith after experiencing a most unimaginable loss. His four wonderful daughters died in a boating accident while they were traveling with their mother to Europe to be with him.

The ship the girls traveled on, the *S.S. Ville du Havre,* was struck by an English vessel and sank in 12 minutes. Two hundred twenty-six people drowned, including Horatio's daughters Tanetta, Maggie, Annie, and Bessie. Their mother was miraculously saved, and she sent word by Western Union to her husband, who was delayed in travel while assisting D. L. Moody and Ira Sankey in a crusade. The short message was: "Saved alone. Your wife."

Horatio Spafford immediately took another ship to join his wife in Cardiff, Wales. It is said that when the ship sailed approximately over the spot where his four daughters lost their lives, he was comforted by these words inspired by the Holy Spirit: "When sorrows like sea billows roll—whatever my lot, Thou has taught me to say, it is well with my soul."

Three years later, in 1876, Philip P. Bliss took this experience and added music. "It Is Well with My Soul" has inspired millions of people. Only by God's grace and His sufficiency could a loving father give meaning to the untimely death of his four daughters.

Life is not always fair, and there aren't always answers to the whys of life. But no matter what, we can sing praises to God for being our source of help and comfort when the waves come into our lives.

PRAYER

*F*ather God, as Your children we pray that during the difficult trials of life we can say, "It is well with my soul." Amen.

ACTION

*P*repare yourself for life's tragedies, and be prepared to say as Horatio Spafford said, "It is well with my soul."

TODAY'S WISDOM

*I*n My Father's house are many dwelling places; if it were not so, I would have told you; for I go to prepare a place for you. If I go and prepare a place for you, I will come again and receive you to Myself, that where I am, there you may be also.

JOHN 14:2-3

The Spirit of Stillness

Cease striving and know that I am God.
PSALM 46:10

*T*he door to stillness is waiting for any of us to open it and go through, but it won't open by itself. We have to choose to make the spirit of stillness a part of our lives. We are bombarded with all the high-tech instruments that cause us to go faster and faster. The drumbeat of today's music wants us to rev up and be louder than ever before. The world tells us to be louder and faster, but God's words are just the opposite: "Be still, and know that I am God."

Nothing helps me understand the stillness of God better than when I'm in a sleeping bag, flat on a hilltop, staring toward heaven, and gazing upon the sky full of stars and a full moon. Then I can grasp the stillness that Scripture talks about.

The complaint I hear from so many women these days is, "I'm just dying for a little peace and quiet—a chance to relax and to think and to pray. And somehow I just can't seem to manage it."

Stillness is not a word that many of us even use anymore, let alone experience. Yet women today, more than at any other time in history, desperately need the spirit of stillness. We are constantly on the move, stretched to our maximum by all the hats we wear, all the balls we juggle, and all the demands our lives bring. In order for the spirit of loveliness to live in us, we must seek opportunities to rest, plan, regroup, and draw closer to God. And we do that when we deliberately cultivate the spirit of stillness in our homes and in our lives.

I would say the ideal balance between outward and inward pursuits should be about 50/50. By *outward* I mean working toward goals and deadlines, negotiating needs and privileges, coping with stress, taking care of daily chores, striving toward retirement—getting things done. Inward things include tuning in to my spiritual self; talking to God; exploring the sorrows, hopes, and dreams that make up the inner me; and just relaxing in God's eternal presence. This would also include physical, mental, and spiritual growth, such as vacations, working out, taking educational classes, and dealing with my inner self.

When I was younger, my life was tilted more outward and less inward. As I grow and mature, I find I'm leaning more toward the inward. I want my life to be geared more toward heaven. I want to spend more time alone with God—talking, reading, listening, and just being—rather than always doing. I want to experience the fragrance of His love and let that love permeate my life, to let the calmness of His Spirit replenish the empty well of my heart, which gets depleted in the busyness and rush of the everyday demands and pressures.

Do whatever is necessary to nurture the spirit of stillness in your life. Don't let the enemy wear you so thin that you lose your balance and perspective. Regular time for stillness is as important and necessary as sleep, exercise, and nutritional food.

Ecclesiastes 3:1 says, "There is an appointed time for everything." That includes a time and a place to cultivate the spirit in the midst of your busy, productive life.

PRAYER

*F*ather God, my desire is to have time for stillness in my busy schedule. I know that a quiet time is so valuable for having good balance in my life. Keep my desire for this discipline a top priority for my daily scheduling. Amen.

ACTION

*I*f you find it difficult to develop a habit of quiet time, find a prayer partner with the same difficulty and hold each other accountable.

TODAY'S WISDOM

*P*rayer, the basic exercise of the spirit, must be actively practiced in our private lives. The neglected soul of man must be made strong enough to assert itself once more. For if the power of prayer is again released and used in the lives of common men and women; if the spirit declares its aims clearly and boldly, there is yet hope that our prayers for a better world will be answered.

ALEXIS CARREL

Foolishness Versus Wisdom

—⫷⫸—

Behold, You desire truth in the innermost
being, and in the hidden part You
will make me know wisdom.

PSALM 51:6

*W*e live in a time when humanity has sold out to secular mate-
rialism. It's a day when many people have put God on hold. The
attitude of "I can do it myself" rules. But as time goes by, many
older people seem to get more wisdom after they find that their
paths have given them little meaning in life. As they ponder mor-
tality, they often realize that the religion they rejected throughout
their youth has meaning and purpose. Fortunate are the people
who adopted fear of God—respect for who God is—at a young
age. They have studied the wisdom of Scripture and applied it to
their value system.

Recently I was driving down one of our busy freeways in southern
California, when a large sign suddenly appeared before me that read:
"Foolish men do in their old age what wise men do in their youth."
This slogan is very true. Wisdom comes from knowing God and
understanding His will for our lives. The Holy Spirit assists us in our
quest for wisdom by enabling us to view the world as God perceives
it. From an early age we can seek God's wisdom. We don't have
to wait until we are old to figure out this puzzle of life. In Psalm
111:10 we read, "The fear of the LORD is the beginning of wisdom;

a good understanding have all those who do His commandments; His praise endures forever."

Don't put off until tomorrow what you can do today. A wasted lifetime is a great loss. Go to the cross of Jesus and trust Him with the simplicity of childlike faith.

PRAYER

*F*ather God, I don't want to wait until I'm old to exhibit Your traits of wisdom. I want a whole life of trusting You and Your Word. May I also be able to share this desire with my family. Bless me as I put my faith in Your hands. Amen.

ACTION

*A*sk God for the wisdom to walk in righteousness.

TODAY'S WISDOM

*T*his is the true joy in life, the being used for a purpose recognized by yourself as a mighty one; the being thoroughly worn out before you are thrown on the scrap heap; the being a force of Nature instead of a feverish selfish little clod of ailments and grievances complaining that the world will not devote itself to making you happy.

GEORGE BERNARD SHAW

Develop a Unique Style

⬥

Create in me a clean heart, O God,
and renew a steadfast spirit within me.

PSALM 51:10

*G*od is a God of creativity and creation. Our cry is to "create in me"…
a loving home, lovely surroundings, a clean heart, honorable children,
a warm family, responsible citizens, a solid marriage—on and on. We
all need to nourish our creative potential. Human beings are expressive
creatures by nature. Many times our past experiences have told us we
aren't. A teacher, a parent, a friend has given us a label of "uncreative."
But in reality, we all have the capacity for great creativity.

There is a freeing, renewing aspect to the Book of Psalms. Let's
use that inspiration from Scripture and discover the unique style
that you can call your own. How do you discover your own unique
decorating style for your home? Here are some tips:

- The first thing you want to do is to look around in all
the shops you can't afford. That sounds like fun, doesn't it?
Visit model homes. Take notes. Make little drawings. Take
a photo if it is appropriate.

- Obtain a variety of decorating magazines. Thumb through
and tear out certain pages that reflect your likings. Make file
folders and label them by headings, such as kitchen, master
bath, pantry, storage closet, etc.

- When finished with this exercise, take a look at what you've selected. You've probably discovered something about your-self. Remember, style isn't what you have. It's what you do with what you have!

Make your home uniquely you. Create a place where you can close the door on a busy day and enjoy a time for you and the Lord. Create a space that welcomes other people and beckons your children to spend time together as a family. Allow your home to become a refuge for you and for everyone who visits.

PRAYER

*C*reator, I know I need less than I think I need. Stir up the creative spirit You've placed within me, and show me how to find You in the simple, ordinary things of my day. Amen.

ACTION

*G*o stir your creative juices today. Try the exercises in the devotion, or sit down with a pad of paper and a marker and plan out a new arrangement for your furniture in one room. Give yourself permission to try new things!

TODAY'S WISDOM

I am only one,
But still I am one.
I cannot do everything,
But still I can do something;
And because I cannot do everything
I will not refuse to do something
that I can do.

EDWARD EVERETT HALE

The Art of Restoration

Restore to me the joy of Your salvation and sustain me with a willing spirit.

PSALM 51:12

𝒥n Psalm 51, David pleads for forgiveness and cleansing (verses 1-2), confesses his guilt (verses 3-6), prays for pardon and restoration (verses 7-12), resolves to praise God (verses 13-17), and prays for the continued prosperity of Jerusalem (verses 18-19). This psalm elaborates David's confession of his sin with Bathsheba (see 2 Samuel 11–12, with emphasis on 12:3).

Psalm 51 highlights the highs of victory and the lows of defeat. As sinners, we all can appreciate how heavy David's heart was and his desire to approach his heavenly Father to ask forgiveness. We can relate to his longing to be restored in his daily walk of uprightness in the presence of God.

Read the complete chapter. This is a confession to meditate over. Take it in and ponder it. Certain words and phrases will surely touch your heart and soul:

- Have mercy on me.
- Blot out my sins.
- I have sinned against You.
- Cleanse me and make me whiter than snow.
- Let me again hear joy and gladness.

- Blot out my iniquity.
- Create in me a pure heart.
- Renew a steadfast spirit within me.
- Restore to me the joy of Your salvation.
- Give me a willing spirit.
- My tongue will sing of Your righteousness.
- Open my lips and mouth for praise.
- Give me a broken and contrite heart.

As we examine this confession, we see a man who has been broken and who begs for restoration. We may have never been to the depths of David's despair, but our sins have brought us to a place where we cry out to God, "Please forgive me, a helpless sinner." These 13 sentences above would be an excellent prayer for any of us who need to pray for forgiveness and restoration. Read each one out loud, as if it is your confession. No sins are too big for God to hear and forgive. Notice that most of these sentences deal with proper attitude. If we approach our prayer time with a proper attitude, the Holy Spirit can do miracles in our lives. As you pray for repentance, believe that you have received it from God.

PRAYER

God, I want to give You all of my known and unknown sins today. I don't want to leave Your presence with any unconfessed sin in my life. Thank You for dying on the cross for me. Amen.

ACTION

Read the complete Fifty-first Psalm.

TODAY'S WISDOM

*I*f my people, who are called by my name, will humble themselves and pray and seek my face and turn from their wicked ways, then I will hear from heaven and will forgive their sin and will heal their land.

2 CHRONICLES 7:14 NIV

The Lord Hears When I Pray

Give ear to my prayer, O God; and do not hide
Yourself from my supplication.

*O*ne of the great promises of Scripture is that, for the children of
God, He always hears us. That's a lifetime guarantee. It's free; we
don't have to pay anything for this extended warranty. The certifi-
cate is the printed Word, the Bible. It's impossible for God not to
keep His Word. If He says it, we can believe it.

As I approach God in either public or private prayer, I must
remember that this is an appointed time between me and my Lord.
I must not flower my speech with babbling words that are mean-
ingless, or ones that puff me up in front of those who hear me talk
with God.

As Jesus shared with His disciples the proper approach to prayer
by giving them the Lord's Prayer (Matthew 6:9-13), we in turn are
exhibiting how to pray for those watching around us. We need to
be humble as we approach and worship the Lord.

During these last few years, I have had the opportunity and
privilege of many, many people praying for me. I have always been
so blessed when those who came to visit asked, "Would you mind
if I prayed for you?" "Of course not," came my immediate reply.

Often the most powerful prayers were those uttered by God-
fearing, humble warriors of the faith. Many of these were people

who have traveled down the same road I traveled. They understood the suffering I was experiencing. They knew the comfort of words that soothe the hurts of any illness. From years of their own suffering taking them to the foot of the cross, they are able to go directly to God. He hears and responds with a blessing. Each petition has an impact upon our heavenly Father. He listens with an open ear to those who are lowly in spirit.

PRAYER

*F*ather God, what would I do without Your attentive ear? You are always there when I need to give my petitions and supplications to You. I appreciate Your interest in my every detail. Amen.

ACTION

*C*ommit to being a prayer warrior for a friend in need.

TODAY'S WISDOM

I have resolved to pray more and pray always, to pray in all places where quietness inviteth, in the house, on the highway, and on the street; and to know no street or passage in this city that may not witness that I have not forgotten God.

SIR THOMAS BROWNE

Sleep and Not Worry

———

Cast your burden upon the LORD and
He will sustain you.

PSALM 55:22

*T*here was this man who owed his next-door neighbor a hundred dollars. The bill was due the next day, and the debtor only had 30 dollars. That night the man was so anxious about the next morning that his tossing and turning kept his wife awake. Finally, exasperated, she got out of bed, threw open the window, and yelled to the neighbor, "Hey, Ruben! About the hundred bucks—he ain't got it! Now," she said to her husband, "let him worry!" And they went to sleep.

Have you ever tossed and turned because you are worrying about some issue in life? Perhaps your child? Your husband? A job? A mistake you made? This worry keeps replaying itself in your head. You fret, lose your train of thought, and become stressed out. Sound familiar? Now when those thoughts creep into your mind, think on today's psalm so you can relax and go to sleep. When God says to cast your burden upon Him and He will sustain you, He means every word of that promise. Remember, God is not capable of breaking His promises.

I have prayed more in the last seven years than I've ever prayed. During this walk with cancer, God and I have become very close. I've meekly prayed, I've prayed with anger, with tears, with a pitched voice, with petitions, with despair, with praise, and of course with thanksgiving. God has heard me each time and has sustained me.

He will sustain you, too. Not only that, He will work out the problem that's plaguing you, no matter what it is. God delights in being our God. Don't rob Him of the joy He gets from shouldering your burden for you. He truly wants to help.

PRAYER

*F*ather God, I want to be more transparent with You regarding my daily problems. You know already what they are. Thanks for being concerned about each and every one. I appreciate You being alongside me. Amen.

ACTION

*C*ast your burdens upon the Lord. Make a list of the worries or fears that cause you the most sleepless nights. Read them aloud to God and hand them over, one by one.

TODAY'S WISDOM

*H*ave courage for the great sorrows of life and patience for the small ones; and when you have laboriously accomplished your daily task, go to sleep in peace. God is awake.

VICTOR HUGO

Tears Become Shouts of Joy

You have taken account of my wanderings;
put my tears in Your bottle; are they
not in Your book?

PSALM 56:8

$\mathcal{T}$here were many days and nights while I was a bone-marrow-transplant patient in Seattle when my pillow was soaked with tears. After a long day of testing as an outpatient, I would return home to our apartment, not knowing what the test results would bring. Each day was a new adventure. At times it seemed like I was on an eternal roller coaster—some days up and some days down. Some days the prognosis was not good, and I would go home and cry. Tears seemed to be my only release for the uncertainties of illness.

The psalmist David was amazed that God was attentive to every detail of his life, even down to the awareness of the tears he shed. So was I. After every tear session, I was comforted to know God was paying attention to my every need. To think that our great God takes notice even of our tears and saves them in His bottle as jewels!

He promises that "they that sow in tears shall reap in joy" (Psalm 126:5 KJV). Our tears will be turned into pearls, precious gems of God. And they are posted in His book of remembrance. He doesn't forget our heartaches. John 11:35 declares that "Jesus wept." Yes, Jesus weeps when we weep. Albert Smith defines *tears* as the safety valves of the heart, releasing pressure when too much stress is laid upon someone. There are various kinds of tears:

- tears of love which burst from our hearts
- tears of sorrow as a mother weeps for her wayward son or daughter
- tears of joy
- tears of compassion
- tears of spiritual desire and hope

My theme through all my trouble is found in Psalm 30:5: "Weeping may last for the night, but a shout of joy comes in the morning." This verse let me see the light at the end of the tunnel. It gave me hope that someday my tears would turn into a shout of joy. I'm now able to continue my writing and speaking schedule. I pretty much can do everything I was previously able to do. Praise God for His abundant grace for my life! My tears have turned to a shout of joy.

PRAYER

*F*ather God, thanks for giving me the hope and assurance that my tears would someday become shouts of joy. You are a great God. Amen.

ACTION

*D*on't be afraid to shed tears when they swell up from your heart. Which kind of tears have you held back? Be willing to release them.

TODAY'S WISDOM

*N*o one is so rich that he does not need another's help; no one so poor as not to be useful in some way to his fellow man; and the disposition to ask assistance from others with confidence, and to grant it with kindness, is part of our very nature.

POPE LEO XIII

Sing Praises unto God

———◦———

My heart is steadfast, O God, my heart
is steadfast; I will sing, yes, I will sing praises!
PSALM 57:7

*H*ave you ever said to God, "You must not understand my situation. See, I've got this and that issue. I've got this and that to do. I have so many responsibilities. Do You really expect me to be quiet, to be confident, and to sing Your praises? I can't do that; I've got too many problems."

Life is full of problems; everyone has far too many troubles that need attention. The Christian life isn't without strife, but we can turn our focus from the problems to praises. I have found when I start the day with God in reading, praying, and praising, my days go much better than when I just head out into the world and forget to spend quiet time with my Lord.

Time management experts tell us that if we do something for 21 consecutive days, we can form a new habit. Start your daily meetings with God today, and then tomorrow begin to wake up with God. You might have to get up 15 to 30 minutes before the rest of the family to do these morning devotions, but you will be amazed at the difference this time alone with Him makes to ease your spirit. You will start your day with a new perspective, less stress, less tension, and fewer problems. Your attitude toward solving these problems will be more relaxed, and your perspective will be refreshed. Surprisingly, people around you will also be better problem solvers because of your new attitude.

PRAYER

*F*ather God, I come to You today with a heart that is quiet and confident. Because of this, You promise to bless my day. Today I have a new beginning. Amen.

ACTION

*S*tart your new 21-day journey. Choose a devotional or a book of the Bible to read through during this habit-development time. Encourage a friend to start this journey on the same day so you can encourage one another.

TODAY'S WISDOM

A famous old violin maker always made his instruments out of wood from the north side of the tree. Why? Because the wood which had endured the brunt of the fierce wind, icy snow, and raging storm lent a finer tone to the violin. In the same way, trouble and sorrow give the soul its sweetest melodies.

A person whose security is in God can be steadfast and unmovable at all times and in any situation. When life seems to crash upon us, we can say, "My soul is bowed down, but my heart is fixed." When we have this security and stability, we can sing a precious song of victory.

AUTHOR UNKNOWN

Counting Sheep Doesn't Work

*I lie awake at night thinking of you—of
how much you have helped me—and how
I rejoice through the night beneath the
protecting shadow of your wings.*

PSALM 63:6-7 TLB

The world tells us to count sheep when we can't sleep. But during the long nighttime hours when I haven't been able to sleep, I've learned to pray and meditate on Scripture. I have found that not only is God the God of the daytime, but He is also the God of the nighttime. Some of my most precious hours come after the sun goes down. The stillness of the evening gives me a wonderful opportunity to pray and meditate on God's holy Word.

When I spend time in the stillness of the night, often I will have a recollection of someone I haven't thought of for a long time. It brings to mind fond memories, but also places that person in my thoughts and prayers. Because I'm in no hurry and don't have any pressing appointments, I can lavishly spend my time praying for that person and his or her family. Often I send a card the next day to let the person know I prayed for him or her.

Perhaps you stay awake at night because there is someone in your life you need to forgive. Holding onto the grace of God, this is possible. We have in Jesus the perfect model of forgiveness and sacrifice as believers. Extend this grace to another, and see how God will change your heart toward that person and the circumstances relating to the reason for forgiveness. If a person doesn't forgive, he or she will remain a prisoner and will live in bondage and not freedom.

Praying for your friends and family is a tremendous privilege. It does your heart good, and it encourages other people to know that you care enough to pray for them. Use your moments of quiet wisely. Consider them a gift, and make room for stillness in your life.

PRAYER

Lord, lead me to pray rather than count sheep when I can't sleep. I will use this quiet time as an opportunity to lift up my family and friends to You. Amen.

ACTION

Let go of the burden you carry today. Forgive someone through a simple prayer to the Lord. Experience this freedom and write about it in your journal.

TODAY'S WISDOM

Do not think that love, in order to be genuine, has to be extraordinary. What we need is to love without getting tired....Be faithful in small things because it is in them that your strength lies.

MOTHER TERESA

Surviving Testing

―――

For You have tried us, O God; You
have refined us as silver is refined.

PSALM 66:10

$\mathcal{S}$t. Francis de Sales said, "We shall steer safely through every storm, so long as our heart is right, our intentions fervent, our courage steadfast, and our trust fixed on God."

When trials come into our lives, we are tempted to ask, "Why, Lord?" Why, Lord, do the righteous suffer? If ever there was a man who loved and obeyed God, it was Job. Yet his testing was very dramatic and even painful. Today all we have to do is pick up the newspaper to read of tragedy touching the just and the unjust.

Everyone has or will experience some kind of tragedy. If not yet, it will come. How we handle these events when they happen is key. There are many wonderful support groups available to help us process our pain. And there are many outlets for us once we are ready to work through our loss, transition, or difficulty.

Whatever your test today is, please know that others have experienced similar pain. Don't go through testing alone. Contact your local church or hospital to find out what programs are available.

Jesus knows and has also experienced our pain. When I think of the pain He suffered on the cross for me, my load seems much lighter. This has given me more courage to fight my battle. He is always with us to help us get through the tough times of life (and we will have some). Trust Him now. Don't wait to prepare. Be ready when those times appear on the horizon.

PRAYER

*F*ather God, I've learned from experience that You are always by my side when the trials of life get stormy and the dark clouds roll overhead. Your rainbow in the sky promises me that things will get better. Amen.

ACTION

*T*urn all your cares over to Jesus and feel secure in His arms. When you pray today, think of yourself resting in God's arms. Consider how safe and secure you feel, and take that feeling with you into your day as you face decisions, concerns, and happiness.

TODAY'S WISDOM

*W*e do not succeed in changing things according to our desire, but gradually our desire changes. The situation that we hoped to change because it was intolerable becomes unimportant. We have not managed to surmount the obstacle, as we were absolutely determined to do, but life has taken us round it, led us past it, and then if we turn round to gaze at the remote past, we can barely catch sight of it, so imperceptible has it become.

MARCEL PROUST

Start Early in Prayer

He has given heed to the voice of my prayer.
PSALM 66:19

$\mathcal{D}$epending on how old your children are, you will soon learn the power of earnest prayer. As Abraham Lincoln said, "I have been driven many times to my knees by the overwhelming conviction that I had nowhere else to go. My own wisdom, and that all about me, seemed insufficient for the day."

As our children got older (now we have grandchildren), my prayer life became stronger. Somehow children bring parents to their knees, especially as those children go through their teen years. During these awkward years, there are so many things that we can't control. Cutting the apron strings is very difficult, particularly for us moms. Somehow dads seem to handle these times a lot better than we moms do. I remember how cool my Bob would stay during very difficult situations. I often commented under my breath that for him to maintain such composure, he surely must not understand the problem.

I always thanked God when I heard the children pull in the driveway at night. Then I knew they were safe. When those little bundles of joy were young, they were so much fun. But as teenagers, they turned into reasons to pray.

Don't wait until they're older to pray diligently for your children or for your nieces, nephews, or neighborhood kids. Start when they come home as babies from the hospital. Every day of their lives they need your prayers to give them protection, a godly walk, a focus on the meaning of life, etc. It's amazing what happens to children when they know that Mom and Dad and other adults are praying every day for them.

PRAYER

*H*eavenly Father, thank You for (each child's name). I love these wonderful human beings You have given me to mother. Remind me daily to keep my children bathed in prayer. Help me to be the exact mother they need to grow into godly adults. Amen.

ACTION

*M*ail a greeting card (preferably handmade) to each of your children, telling them how much you love them. Children love to receive mail, even from Mom, who lives in the same house.

TODAY'S WISDOM

*T*he time and the quality of the time that their parents devote to them indicate to children the degree to which they are valued by their parents.

M. SCOTT PECK

Be Alert to Life

Blessed be the Lord, who daily loads us with
benefits, the God of our salvation!
PSALM 68:19 NKJV

$\mathcal{M}$y good friend Florence Littauer has always encouraged me and her audiences to be alert to life. Pay attention to the events around you; continually read to know the current events around the world. She is always sending me newspaper and magazine articles dealing with my areas of expertise in life. She truly is my example of someone who notices her daily blessings from God.

I don't understand people who are not excited about life. It amazes me that some people find life dull and boring. They must not be seeing and hearing the same life that I am. Going through cancer has made me more appreciative of all that life has to offer. Each morning is a miracle for me, and I never want to take any day for granted. Even my not-so-good days are exciting because I'm still alive to enjoy those days, too. All you have to do is look around and observe, watch, look, and listen. Everything in sight is in some way a blessing from God. Honestly, He is daily giving me more blessings than I can receive. Truly my cup overflows.

When I realize that the ray of sunlight I see is there for me, I say, "Thank You." When the trees wave their branches, I say, "Thank You, Lord." The birds that sing, the fruits, the vegetables, and the blooming flowers are also just for me, and I say, "Thank You." All these things are also just for you. Have you stopped to take notice—to appreciate the beauty and the gift of the new beginning every day presents?

The smiles we receive, the hand extended in welcome, the hugs that warm us, and the compliments that enter our ears are all blessings from God. Blue skies, rain clouds, friends, great books, delicious food, beautiful flowers are from His bountiful heart. All that we have to do to receive these is open our senses to find this exciting life. Every day God is so good.

PRAYER

God, don't let me take anything for granted. Let me open my eyes each day and take in all the benefits You have given me. Amen.

ACTION

Pay attention to the life around you today! Teach your family how to love life and to be thankful.

TODAY'S WISDOM

Eternal joy is the end of the ways of God. The message of all religions is that the Kingdom of God is peace and joy. And it is the message of Christianity. But eternal joy is not to be reached by living on the surface. It is rather attained by breaking through the surface, by penetrating the deep things of ourselves, of our world, and of God. The moment in which we reach the last depth of our lives is the moment in which we can experience the joy that has eternity within it, the hope that cannot be destroyed, and the truth on which life and death are built. For in the depth is truth; and in the depth is hope; and in the depth is joy.

PAUL TILLICH

Slow Down

—◁▩▷—

And do not hide Your face from Your servant,
for I am in distress; answer me quickly.
PSALM 69:17

Don't be like David and wait until the floor falls out from under you before you call upon God. We wait and wait for our problems to fester or our hurts to pile up, and then when things explode into chaos or emergencies, we want God to work everything out immediately. When I became sick, I just wanted to get well fast. I thought, "Give me the chemo and radiation, and in a few months I will be back to my usual routine of life." I didn't mind being sick for a little while, because I knew the doctors and pharmacists had enough skill to solve my problems.

The truth is, God did rescue me—but in His time, not at my hurried pace. After seven long years of treatment, there are no signs of cancer in my body. I certainly appreciate God's loving patience.

I often pray for God to keep me humble. Well, He is doing that. I appreciate what God is doing in my life. He has put a strong desire in my soul to spend time every day with Him. I respond, "Let time stand still, and let me forget all about my busy schedule. I want to keep my focus on the Lord."

PRAYER

*L*ord, the world wants You to act swiftly, but I've learned that Your clock moves slower than my watch. Let me learn to adjust to Your timetable and not mine. Amen.

ACTION

*S*et your watch to move at the same pace as God's clock. Check yourself and your mind-set as you go about your day today. When you are impatient, breathe deeply and give that moment to God. What or who can you think about, pray about while you practice God's pace?

TODAY'S WISDOM

*U*se your trials. What is the purpose of the testing? God makes our trials the instrument of blessing. Too often our trials work impatience, but God will give grace that His real purpose may be accomplished. Patience is more necessary than anything else in our faith life. We forget that time is nothing with God, for with Him a thousand years is as one day, and one day as a thousand years. Christ's purpose in our lives is that we shall be perfect and entire, wanting nothing.

HENRIETTA MEARS

The Other Side of Hardships

For I was envious of the arrogant as I saw the
prosperity of the wicked.

PSALM 73:3

$\mathcal{I}$t seems like the new trend is to be mad at the rich and be suspicious of how they made their money. Surely the rich had to be shady characters, or they couldn't be wealthy. When I was growing up in a low-middle-class family, I never remember being so class-conscious. I knew there were rich kids around me, but I certainly wasn't envious. That was just the way life was. But today the class warfare is polarizing our country.

As David was looking around, he must have felt this same envy, and he couldn't understand the injustice of the wicked and their prosperity. I, too, sometimes look around and see the unrighteous prospering and living to ripe old ages, while the good people are struck down with illnesses at a young age, or they experience more economic hardships or natural disasters like floods, tornadoes, hurricanes, and earthquakes.

Why? Why? Doesn't it seem unfair? Yes it does, but one thing I have learned about life: It isn't fair. How do we respond to these incongruities?

- We can cast away our faith and become skeptics.
- We can accept that there are dual forces at work that we can't do anything about; we just accept the fate of each.

- We can deny the existence of evil and accept only that which is good.
- We can realize that we have a sovereign God who, in time, will grant us understanding.

I choose the last thought, knowing that in the past God has used hardships to discipline my life. God has been loving and just in His dealings with me. He will be the same with you! Life's pains and sorrows are necessary refining influences to make us more Christlike.

PRAYER

*G*od, please help me to understand when I get frustrated with life. Let me look not to my left or to my right, but upward in my time of need. Amen.

ACTION

*T*rust God with your pain and suffering.

TODAY'S WISDOM

*C*onsider it all joy, my brethren, when you encounter various trials, knowing that the testing of your faith produces endurance. And let endurance have its perfect result, so that you may be perfect and complete, lacking in nothing.

JAMES 1:2-4

Have I Ever Seen a Christian?

*We will not conceal them [God's
commandments] from their children, but tell to
the generation to come the praises of
the LORD, and His strength and His wondrous
works that He has done.*

PSALM 78:4

*O*ne evening a young father was having a discussion with his young son as they were preparing for bed. The father had been reading one of the lad's stories from the previous Sunday school lesson. Dad was explaining how Christians should act. When he finished sharing his thoughts, the son looked into his father's eyes and asked, "Daddy, have I ever seen a Christian?" The father, disheartened by the question, thought, *What kind of an example am I?*

What would your response be if one of your children asked you the same question? In our verse for today, we are given some help to make sure this doesn't happen. The writer of Psalm 78 states we can do this by:

- sharing with the next generation God's commandments
- giving praises to God for what He has done in the past, the present, and the future

Hopefully and prayerfully, our children will see by our example and words that we are Christians. In Deuteronomy 6:6-7 Moses said, "These words, which I am commanding you today, shall be on your heart. You shall teach them diligently to your sons and shall talk of them when you sit in your house and when you walk by the way and when you lie down and when you rise up."

As parents, we are to be a reflection of God to our children. As these young children look into our faces, our lives, they are to see a man or woman of godly desires and actions. Today we earnestly need more parents who will stand up and be counted to do the right thing.

Christian growth is a daily process of taking off the old self of attitudes, beliefs, and behaviors which reflect the dark side of our nature (sin) and changing to those characteristics that reflect the presence of Christ in our lives. We cannot do this changing by our own power. The only way we can grow and succeed in this continuous growth process is by being renewed in the spirit of our minds (Ephesians 4:22-24). It is a moment-to-moment process. We put away the old self and put on the new self, which in the likeness of God has been created in righteousness and holiness of the truth.

By word and by personal example, we must train and nurture our children. They will know what a Christian is because they know you—the reflector of God's grace.

PRAYER

*F*ather God, thank You for giving me Your commandments, which give me knowledge of who You are and what You expect out of life. As a parent, may I be able to live that out in my everyday life so that those around me can see Jesus. Amen.

ACTION

*S*ay a prayer today with your children, thanking God for all your blessings.

TODAY'S WISDOM

Don't count how many years
you've spent,
Just count the good
you've done;
The times you've lent
a helping hand,
The friends that you have won.
Count your deeds of kindness,
The smiles, not the tears;
Count all the pleasures
that you've had,
But never count the years.

AUTHOR UNKNOWN

Fill My Cup, Lord

My soul longed and even yearned for the courts
of the LORD; my heart and my flesh sing
for joy to the living God.

PSALM 84:2

*O*ften I have this great urge to sing for joy when I'm in church. I love how God speaks to me in songs of praise.

One of my favorite gospel songs is "Fill My Cup, Lord." The message of that song has been dear to my heart for years. One of my favorite books that I have penned is entitled the same, *Fill My Cup, Lord*. Richard Blanchard Sr.'s song asks God to quesnch his thirst and make him whole...to fill his cup overflowing.

Long before I began my collection of lovely china teacups, years before my first child was born, before my writing and speaking ministry seemed to be a possibility, something deep in my spirit echoed the cry of that song. Little did I know then how life can truly drain us. Today I know more.

"Fill my cup" remains the constant cry of my thirsty heart. As we mature and find the responsibilities and pressures mounting, this simple prayer can mean the difference between operating on empty and having a cup that runs over for those we love and serve.

I'm imagining you today with a cup of tea beside you and a quiet moment that you've managed to carve out of your day. Just for a moment there are no ringing phones or crying children. Come as you are, cup in hand! It's so simple. "Fill my cup, Lord." Only when your cup is full are you able to give to other people. An empty cup can offer no relief for those who need refreshing. Don't let the negative thoughts come forth. There is no comfort in negative words. Only positive thoughts are a balm that heals.

PRAYER

*L*ord, I am empty without You. I bring my empty cup and my open heart before Your throne. You are the great Giver. Fill my cup, Lord, that I may pour out Your life on others. Amen.

ACTION

*E*mpty your dirty cup at the cross, and fill it with the freshness that the cross gives you in Jesus' life.

TODAY'S WISDOM

*L*ORD, you have assigned me my portion and my cup; you have made my lot secure. The boundary lines have fallen for me in pleasant places; surely I have a delightful inheritance.

PSALM 16:5-6 NIV

Standing in the House of God

⸺◦⸺

I would rather stand at the threshold
of the house of my God, than dwell in the
tents of wickedness.

PSALM 84:10

*W*hen we were first married and for many years after, we were gatherers and accumulators of material things. We were always looking for a new piece of furniture, an upgrade appliance, and the latest kitchen gadget. Gather, gather, gather, always gathering. However, as we have gotten older, we've realized that life is more than things. Now we find ourselves giving away or selling items that once meant so much to us.

After living 18 years at the "Barnes' Barn," we needed to move closer to my oncologist 45 miles away. In preparation for the move, we had to go through all of our possessions and sort out what to keep, sell, give away, or throw away. It wasn't easy. After 44 years accumulating special items for our home and receiving gifts from beloved friends, our things had helped create a home that was welcoming and comfortable.

Deciding what to part with involved a lot of thought and several strolls down memory lane as we recalled who gave us what or where we had bought a favorite item. While the memories were fun, we realized that accumulating things is not what's important. These things are temporal possessions. The eternal things we leave as our legacy are so much more important.

Our sorting experience brought to mind another couple who also held a garage sale because they were moving to a smaller home. One of their possessions was a journal of sayings this couple had collected that reflected their thoughts about life.

One section was called "We Leave Our Children." It read:

We leave our children...

- *The most precious of all gifts—familial, brotherly, and spiritual love*
- *Self-reliance, courage, conviction, and respect for self and others*
- *A sense of humor or else life will be a bitter teacher*
- *A will to work—for work well done brings pride and joy*
- *A talent for sharing—for society needs belief in individual worth*
- *The passion of truth—for truth is a straight answer, the beginning of trust*
- *The lantern of hope—which lights the dark corners of the mind*
- *The knowledge of belonging*
- *Impromptu praise*
- *A soft caress*
- *A sense of wonder at the things of nature*
- *A love of friends without reciprocity*
- *The size of God's Word, in print so small it fits inside each heart, in meaning so great it spreads over the earth*

AUTHOR UNKNOWN

PRAYER

Lord, in life we must sort out what to keep, what to sell, and what to give away. Give me the wisdom to know what's important in Your eyes. Amen.

ACTION

*H*ave a garage sale of your mind. Weed out what to keep and what to give away and what to avoid gathering in the future!

TODAY'S WISDOM

*W*e are given one day to spend at each morn,
And what we do with this God-given gift
   Will determine whether we are reborn
Or just waste away the sands that do sift.

   So aim at the real treasures of man.
Think not about money or power or gain.
Rather, use the precious moments you can
And glory in Time, ere it slip by and wane.

RICHARD B. BROWN

I Can Do That

For the LORD *God is a sun and shield; the*
LORD *gives grace and glory; no good thing does*
He withhold from those who walk uprightly.
PSALM 84:11

$\mathcal{W}$hen I thumb through all the home-design magazines or see one of those house makeover shows on television, I get overwhelmed by the thought of the costs involved. I catch myself throwing up my hands and saying, "I can't do that!" However, I've found that being realistic can be a very spiritual exercise. I have to exercise faith to look life straight in the eye at times and declare, "This is the way it is!" Other times, though, the correct response is to look beyond those limitations and dream about how life is meant to be lived.

Today I suggest that you not let a small budget keep you from dreaming. You don't have to say, "I can't do that!" If you love a custom look, but you don't have a custom budget, consider a "semi-designer" approach: Use a professional to help you get the right pieces, then decorate the rest of the room on your own. Enjoy the process. Be patient. You'll get where you want to go. Or go back to those magazines and shows and create your own unique look by pulling ideas from here and there. Become a designer!

Our version of goodness or even greatness is often distorted by what other people are doing or the life someone else is living. Don't miss out on the beauty and potential that surrounds you, and I don't just mean in your home's decor. I mean in life! God does not have the restrictions we place on ourselves. If you are facing a hurdle or a transition and are worried about making it through, say, "I can do that...with God!"

PRAYER

Father God, help me sort through my priorities so that they might reflect Your dreams for me. Your simple, majestic love is enough for me today. Amen.

ACTION

Face your dreams and your challenges by saying, "I can do it with God!"

TODAY'S WISDOM

I wish you could truly begin the study of God. This must be our delight throughout eternity. It is the happiest and most helpful study that can possibly engage our thoughts. Why cannot we know God without study? Because all knowledge is thus acquired. To learn a thing without study is to forget it. To learn and not use, is also to forget. Life is unhappy to many because they know so little of God. Those who know Him best are most anxious to know more of Him.

DAVID C. COOK, *The Secret of Happy Home-Life* (1898)

Bloom Where You Are Planted

Indeed, the LORD will give what is good;
and our land will yield its produce.

PSALM 85:12

*F*lowers always lift my spirits. Their delightful colors and interesting shapes and lovely scents can stir a heart of gratitude in every woman I know. Over the years I've been blessed with having an abundance of beautiful flowers in our home. My Bob has always loved gardening; regardless of the season, our yard overflowed with a variety of flowers. Their very presence influences my soul and spirit.

Fresh flowers are such a simple way of saying, "I cherish my home." You don't need a dozen roses from the florist. A bunch of daisies from the supermarket or an iris from your yard can proclaim, "Love lives here."

Do you realize that God has planted you right where you are? Oh, there will still be change ahead. You can be sure of that. But God has planted you in your situation, in your relationships, in your home, in your circumstances so that you can blossom into a woman who says, "God's love lives here" with her words, actions, and beauty.

Take in the abundance and aroma of daily living. Let's be as flowers and allow the joy and peace of our Lord to permeate the walls of our homes and the rooms of our lives with a spirit of loveliness that only Christ Himself can give.

PRAYER

*G*od, I see Your gentle touch on my life each day. You are the master Gardener, tending to the garden of my soul. Thank You. The beauty You are creating is a delight. Amen.

ACTION

*C*ut some fresh flowers today and adorn your dining room table. Let them remind you of what God is doing in your life and through all of your circumstances.

TODAY'S WISDOM

*T*here is only one thing about which I shall have no regrets when my life ends. I have savored to the full all the small, daily joys. The bright sunshine on the breakfast table; the smell of the air at dusk; the sound of the clock ticking; the light rains that start gently after midnight; the hour when the family come home; Sunday-evening tea before the fire! I have never missed one moment of beauty, not ever taken it for granted. Spring, summer, autumn, or winter. I wish I had failed as little in other ways.

AGNES SLIGH TURNBULL

The Doxology

*I will give thanks to You, O Lord
my God, with all my heart, and will glorify
Your name forever.*

PSALM 86:12

*T*he other Sunday my family was attending our early-morning church service. When the "Doxology" appeared on the two large screens in the front of the auditorium, the whole congregation instantly began to lift their voices to robustly sing these words: "Praise God from whom all blessings flow; praise Him, all creatures here below; praise Him above, ye heavenly host; praise Father, Son, and Holy Ghost. Amen." My soul was lifted high, and I was so glad that my family could rejoice with me. The power of those words to inspire, inspired me to find out more about that song.

The following week I went to one of my reference books on early church music and found this account behind the writing of this great song of the church.

> The lines of the "Doxology" have been the most frequently sung words of any known song for more than 300 years. Even today most English-speaking Protestant congregations unite at least once each Sunday in this noble overture of praise. It has been said that the Doxology has done more to teach the doctrine of the Trinity than all the theology books ever written.

Instead of being merely a hymn that is sung periodically, the Doxology should be regarded by Christians as an offering or sacrifice of praise to God for all His blessings from the past week (Hebrews 13:15).[5]

Consider the blessings that flow from God's heart to your life, and praise Him for such goodness. Do you realize that the difficulties in your life should be counted as blessings as well? When you lift those up to God in prayer during your time of need, also thank Him for what He is doing in your life. Keep your spirit of praise throughout the day, for it will brighten and inspire your journey.

PRAYER

Father God, I sing this "Doxology" as a prayer of commitment to You. I want to always praise You—Father, Son, and Holy Ghost—in word, song, and deed. Amen.

ACTION

In your best shower voice, sing the "Doxology."

TODAY'S WISDOM

Teach us, good Lord, to serve Thee as Thou deservest:
To give and not to count the cost;
To fight and not to heed the wounds;
To toil and not to seek for rest;
To labor and not to ask for any reward,
save that of knowing that we do Thy will,
Through Jesus Christ our Lord.
Amen.

St. Ignatius of Loyola

Truths That Keep Their Promises

*But You, O Lord, are a God merciful
and gracious, slow to anger and abundant in
lovingkindness and truth.*

PSALM 86:15

The world is searching for truth. We look everywhere. Our magazines, television, commercials, newspapers, and politicians are supposed to be truth-tellers, but many of them are exposed for their lack of honesty. Never in my life have I been exposed to so much news about people who are supposed to tell the truth, but are on trial on charges that they weren't being honest to their company and their shareholders.

Fortunately I know one truth-teller who is never wrong: the Trinity—God the Father, God the Son, and God the Holy Spirit. If any one of these tells you something, you can believe it because they aren't capable of telling a lie.

Below are some promises that you can trust and act on:

- Call unto me, and I will answer thee (Jeremiah 33:3 KJV).
- The grass withers and the flowers fall, but the word of our God stands forever (Isaiah 40:8 NIV).
- Lead me in thy truth, and teach me; for thou art the God of my salvation; on thee do I wait all the day (Psalm 25:5 KJV).
- Now therefore, go, and I will be with your mouth and teach you what you shall say (Exodus 4:12 NKJV).

- And the LORD shall guide thee continually…and thou shalt be like a watered garden, and like a spring of water, whose waters fail not (Isaiah 58:11 KJV).

When you are trying to figure out who is or isn't speaking truth, ask this simple question: "Which one agrees with the promises of Scripture?" Turn to God's Word to compare what you are hearing to His truth. The more time you spend in Scripture, the more discerning you will be as you make choices, face big and small decisions, and try to live a righteous life.

PRAYER

*F*ather God, I always know that I'm going to hear the truth when I come to You in prayer or when I read Your inspired Word. Thank You for being a promise-keeper. Amen.

ACTION

*B*e known as a truth-teller.

TODAY'S WISDOM

*T*he story goes that a father found a favorite cherry tree hacked and ruined. He cried sternly to his son, "George, who did this?" The son looked at his father with a quivering lip and said, "Father, I can't tell a lie. I did it." "Alas!" said the father, "my beautiful tree is ruined; but I would rather lose all the trees I have than have a liar for my son." The boy who feared a lie more than punishment became the hero and first president of his country, the great General George Washington.

AMERICAN LEGEND

Live for Today

*Blessed are those who have learned to
acclaim you, who walk in the light of
your presence, O LORD.*
PSALM 89:15 NIV

*Y*esterday is gone and tomorrow hasn't come. All we have is today. I
don't know about you, but I'm always looking forward to tomorrow.
At my age, I'm still learning how to live for today. Children often ask
questions to clarify future plans: "Do we go to the beach on Saturday?
Will we go to the park tomorrow?" They want to advance the clock
to the future and be certain that things will turn out as planned. As
adults we do the same thing, and we spend time worrying about
tomorrow's uncertainties rather than celebrating today's certainties.

Today is not just an ordinary day. It's one like no other day we
have lived. "This is the day the LORD has made; let us rejoice and be
glad in it" (Psalm 118:24 NIV). No matter if it's raining, snowing,
blowing, or boiling, we need to rejoice and be glad in this day. Let's
do something special:

- Make a new meal or clothes item.
- Stroll through the park.
- Fly a kite with the children.
- Paint the bathroom.
- Clean out the front closet.

Today is an amazing day. God has created new opportunities that did not exist yesterday and will not exist tomorrow. So let's celebrate this time. Let's read a poem, write a poem, write a song, or sing a song of praise. God delights in showering us with His very special blessings. "Every good and perfect gift is from above, coming down from the Father of the heavenly lights, who does not change like shifting shadows" (James 1:17 NIV).

Today is a special day because we realize that God freely offers us His best gifts to enjoy. In John 10:10 (NIV) Jesus states, "I have come that they may have life, and have it to the full." God wants us to have a full and abundant life. He has spread a banquet before us. Today is that feast. We have to participate in order to taste the food. If you watch from the sideline, you won't be able to taste the abundance that He has given us.

Let's thank God for this free gift of life. Let's praise Him for who He is. Let's trust Him for the days to come. This abundant life fills the God void in our lives, and it also provides us with power to overcome the problems of life. Decide to live out today fully and wholly and with great expectations.

PRAYER

Lord, let me rejoice in this day You have given me. I want to count Your blessings. Let me look at today as a gift from You. May I be a good steward of every hour. I want to rejoice and be glad in this day. Amen.

ACTION

Do something special today. What might it be?

TODAY'S WISDOM

Thank You, God,
for a quiet place
far from life's
crowded ways,
where our hearts
find true contentment
and our souls
fill up with praise.

AUTHOR UNKNOWN

What Is Home?

*LORD, You have been our dwelling
place in all generations.*

PSALM 90:1

"I long to see home," says the sailor when the ship rocks to and fro from the violence of the storm. "I am going home," thinks the shopkeeper when he bars his heavy doors and closes his windows at night, tired from the labors of the day. "I must hurry home," says the mother whose heart is on her baby in the cradle. "Don't stop me; I am going home," says the bright-eyed girl skipping along the footpath. And "almost home," says the dying Christian. "I shall soon be home, and then no more sorrow nor sighing forever. Almost home."

As Dorothy said in *The Wizard of Oz*, "There's no place like home!" In each of our hearts there is a yearning for home. When we are returning from a trip, my heart beats with excitement, because I'm getting close to that wonderful place called home.

We all need a place where we can unwind and regroup, where we can get in touch with who we are and what God has planned for us. In our busy lives, home is just as important as it always has been, and maybe more so. Home is as much a state of the heart and spirit as it is a specific place. It doesn't take a lot of money or even a lot of time to make a welcoming refuge. What it does require is a determination to think beyond necessities and go for what enriches the soul.

A home is where real life happens. But it doesn't happen all at once! It's a lifelong, step-by-step process of discovery. It has taken me more than 45 years to develop the systems that help me maintain order, and I'm still learning. Many things that are truly important in life take a little extra time. Let God use you to bring a sense of comfort and welcome to a troubled world. Important, indeed!

There are lots of voices trying to tell us how to achieve the happy, healthy lifestyles we all desire. But remember, it starts with home.

PRAYER

Lord, thank You for the gift of my home. I pray today that Your presence in my home and in my life will be apparent to each person who comes within these walls. Amen.

ACTION

Start changing your house into a home.

TODAY'S WISDOM

To Adam, paradise was home. To the good among his descendants, home is paradise.

ITALIAN PROVERB

Day by Day

*Teach us to number our days and recognize how few
they are; help us to spend them as we should.*

PSALM 90:12 TLB

If we can control our days, we can control our destiny. That's
how some people think, but in reality we have little control over
anything. God knows the beginning from the end. He has ordained
each of our days and wants us to realize they are few in number.
Some of us have fewer than others. As a young girl, I couldn't
wait until certain things occurred. I would count down the days
until my birthday, the start of school, the start of Passover. But
as an adult, we focus on years. How long we have lived in a particular house. How many anniversaries we have celebrated with our
spouse. How old we are. How long until retirement.

Today's verse suggests that we are to number our days. We are
encouraged to live each day to the fullest so that, when our life
draws to an end, we have gained "a heart of wisdom" or spent each
day as we should. When we live each day unto the Lord, we live it
with gusto and enthusiasm for Him. Our feet should be excited to
touch the floor. We're raring to start the day without a falter in our
step or our enthusiasm.

I have found that, as I get older, inevitable things happen, and
I must learn to adjust to these unknowns that appear from time to
time. I cannot do this in years, but only from day to day and often

hour to hour. Aging isn't a choice. It just happens. All of us will get old if we live long enough.

Celebrate the life God has given you. Art Linkletter said, "Cranky old people were probably cranky young people." This is so true in most instances. Live each day unto the glory of God. Let Him respond when you meet, "Well done, good and faithful servant."

PRAYER

Father, You have given me this day. May I live it to Your glory. Let my response to life be an encouragement to those around me. You give me purpose. Amen.

ACTION

Live today to the fullest—no negative responses allowed.

TODAY'S WISDOM

He has not promised we will never feel lonely,
But He has promised that in Him
We will never be alone.
He has not promised that we will be free
From pain and sorrow,
But He has promised He will be our help,
Our strength, our everlasting peace.
No matter what happens in our lives,
We can believe fully in His promise…
We can rest confidently in His love.

AUTHOR UNKNOWN

Your Work Has Worth

Confirm for us the work of our hands;
yes, confirm the work of our hands.
PSALM 90:17

*W*omen are continually confronted with the idea that being a home-maker is pretty simple, and if you really had skills, you would have an out-of-the-home job. I had a lady tell me at a recent seminar that her husband demanded that she get an outside job that paid money. When she presented her case for staying home, he replied, "You're just taking the easy way out." I couldn't believe that a husband would think that being a homemaker was taking the easy way out.

For many years I struggled to acknowledge worth in my work as a homemaker. I didn't have a college degree, and I was a home-maker with five children. I was always tired, with little energy for anything else—including romancing my husband. I didn't have a good handle on who I was as a person. My self-talk was filled with phrases like "You aren't worth much," "You don't have a career," "Your job is so mundane," "Anyone could do what you do," and "I'm stuck with no place to go."

Over and over these negative thoughts went through my head. As you can suspect, I wasn't very exciting to be around. Thankfully, during this period in my life I was involved in a small Bible study with older, godly women who shared two passages of scripture that changed my life.

One was Proverbs 31, which talked about the virtuous woman,

and the other was Titus 2:4-5, which describes a wife's core roles as "husband lover" and "child lover." These two sections of Scripture gave me the tools I needed to establish proper priorities in my life roles and for my decisions. I soon realized that this whole concept of work and worth was very complex, and that each woman and each family has to determine what is best for them, using biblical guidelines.

As I looked at the Titus passage, I realized that God wanted me to be a lover of my husband and children and to be a maker of my home. This was refreshing to me because I had looked at all these drudgeries as an end unto themselves, not as a means to fulfilling one of my primary roles as a woman. Now I found my attitude toward this work changing. I was beginning to do it out of love rather than obligation.

When I changed my focus, I realized what today's verse was addressing when it says, "Confirm for us the work of our hands." What's in it for me as a wife and mother? "Her children rise up and bless her; her husband also, and he praises her, saying: 'Many daughters have done nobly, but you excel them all'" (Proverbs 31:28-29).

PRAYER

*F*ather God, push away all the negative thoughts that attack my worth. Let me learn from Your Word about the worth I have in You. Amen.

ACTION

*W*rite in your journal what God has done to confirm your worth.

TODAY'S WISDOM

In this life you sometimes have to choose between pleasing God and pleasing man. In the long run it's better to please God—He's more likely to remember.

HARRY KEMELMAN

How to Live Longer

—◦—

With a long life I will satisfy him and
let him see My salvation.
PSALM 91:16

$\mathcal{I}$n America we are going through major changes in our health and medical insurance programs. The medical profession itself is not what it used to be because big changes have been made and more are to come. Healthcare is a major political issue. How are we going to take care of the sick, and who will pay for these services?

It is well-known in the medical profession that an amazingly large percentage of human disease and suffering is directly traceable to worry, fear, conflict, immorality, dissipation, unwholesome thinking, and unclean living. If people would pursue godly living, their lives would be much healthier and much of the illness we find in America and throughout the world would be wiped out.

The Bible associates health, prosperity, and longevity with godliness. Godliness does lead to blessings, even during dark times. My doctors tell me that patients with faith have a higher degree and rate of survival than those without faith. The proper attitude brings healing. If we place our trust in God, we can look for His favor in our lives.

PRAYER

*F*ather God, Your principles of life work in all issues of life. Those who put their trust and faith in You are much healthier than those who don't. I appreciate You extending to me a richer and fuller life. Amen.

ACTION

*G*od says He will give us a long life if we strive for godliness. How are you going to use your days?

TODAY'S WISDOM

*T*hese trials are only to test your faith, to see whether or not it is strong and pure. It is being tested as fire tests gold and purifies it—and your faith is far more precious to God than mere gold; so if your faith remains strong after being tried in the test tube of fiery trials, it will bring you much praise and glory and honor on the day of his return.

1 Peter 1:7 tlb

Each Day Is Precious

*Declare Your lovingkindness in the morning
and Your faithfulness by night.*

PSALM 92:2

Your quiet time is not a gift you give God, but a gift that God gives you. Rather than offering Him your quiet time, simply offer Him yourself. We don't have to be eloquent with our words, powerful with our writing, handsome in our appearance. Sure, those are helpful, but He will mold you and shape you into the person He wants you to be. All we have to say when we are called is, "Here I am. Take me and use me in Thy own way."

Get in the habit of saying, "Good morning, Lord" and "Good evening, Lord." This practice will give you joy in the morning and peace at night. Start and end each day with some time of simply being with God. Be still in His presence before bringing all your petitions and concerns. Greet God with adoration, awe, and respect. He is not some man upstairs or a gray-haired father figure; He is our heavenly Father.

Remember and be thankful for the prayers He has answered in the past. Let all your praying be preceded by praise. We must remember that in the authority of Jesus' name, we can expect answers to our prayers. "All things you ask in prayer, believing, you will receive" (Matthew 21:22). We can be courageous in our asking and confident in His answers. We have the privilege of celebrating God's presence, for His faithfulness is both a promise and a blessing.

I never want to take for granted the beginning of a new day or the ending of that day. Each day should be received and appreciated as a gift.

PRAYER

*F*ather God, as You are the Alpha and the Omega—the beginning and the end—I want to start and end each day with Your praises. Help me to be focused on all You have done, are doing, and will do in the future for me. Amen.

ACTION

*S*et a goal to start and end each day this month praising God.

TODAY'S WISDOM

*P*ersonal prayer, it seems to me, is one of the simplest necessities of life, as basic to the individual as sunshine, food and water—and at times, of course, more so. By prayer I believe we mean an effort to get in touch with the Infinite. We know that our prayers are imperfect. Of course they are. We are imperfect human beings. A thousand experiences have convinced me beyond room of doubt that prayer multiplies the strength of the individual and brings within the scope of his capabilities almost any conceivable objective.

DWIGHT D. EISENHOWER

Take Time to Say Thank You

For You, O LORD, hast made me glad
by what You have done, I will sing for joy
at the works of Your hands.

PSALM 92:4

*J*ulian of Norwich said so well, "A cheerful giver does not count the cost of what he gives. His heart is set on pleasing and cheering him to whom the gift is given." When we were raising our children, we were careful to teach them good manners, including saying "thank you." When they received a present or compliment, we couldn't wait for them to say the two magic words before we would blurt out, "What do you say?" With bright eyes, they would answer, "Thank you." We have continued the tradition with our grandchildren. It's wonderful when they mature to the point where they don't have to be reminded to be thankful. I'm sure that God waits for us to show signs of thankfulness for all He's done for us. We were created to have fellowship with God; the chief end of man is to know God, enjoy Him, and thank Him.

Saying "thank you" makes everybody feel a little bit more appreciated. I know that my mom loved to hear from my brother and me, "Momma, this was a very good dinner. Thank you!"

When we receive a lot of attention because of our situation in life, we must remember our good manners and say "thank you." During the lowest point of my illness, I didn't have the energy to write or call a "thank you" to my blessed angels who sent cards, flowers, food, etc. However, my Bob spent hours each week sending off thank-you cards and notes. He typed up a handprint letter with a note saying "thank you." Then he mailed them off to dear ones who contributed to my wellness.

As we look at all of God's creation, we need to voluntarily face skyward and say, "Thank You."

PRAYER

Lord, may I have the maturity to appreciate You and express that appreciation to You. Each day, by Your grace, I experience the pleasures of Your creation. I am so grateful for this life. Amen.

ACTION

Write or call someone today and express a spirit of thanksgiving.

TODAY'S WISDOM

Thou that hast given so much to me,
give one thing more—a grateful heart;
not thankful when it pleaseth me,
as if Thy blessing had spare days,
but such a heart whose pulse may be Thy praise.

GEORGE HERBERT

Near to the Heart of God

———

*When my anxious thoughts multiply within
me, Your consolations delight my soul.*

PSALM 94:19

*L*ife is often filled with unexpected problems and crises. Unrest
and despair will darken the way of even the strongest saint. Yet the
Christian, because of the refuge he has in God, should strive to
maintain composure and stability in spite of stress and difficulties.
We cannot escape the pressures and dark shadows in our lives, but
they can be faced with a spiritual strength that our Lord provides.
As we are held securely "near to the heart of God," as a favorite
hymn of mine states, we find the rest, the comfort, the joy, and
peace that only Jesus our Redeemer can give. Because of this, we
can live every day with an inner calm and courage.

This is the message that Cleland McAfee expressed in this
consoling hymn at a time when his own life was filled with
sadness. While he was serving as a pastor of the First Presby-
terian Church in Chicago, Dr. McAfee was stunned to hear
the shocking news that his two beloved nieces had just died
from diphtheria. Turning to God and the Scriptures, McAfee
soon felt the lines and the tune of this new hymn flow from
his grieving heart. On the day of the double funeral, he
stood outside the quarantined home of his brother Howard
singing these words as he choked back the tears.

The following Sunday the hymn was repeated by the choir of McAfee's church. It soon became widely known and has since ministered comfort and spiritual healing to many of God's people in times of need.[6]

PRAYER

*F*ather God, I know how You hold the sick and distressed in Your comforting arms. I have been in such a place, and Your reassurances are what have given me the desire to live. Amen.

ACTION

*S*ing the words from this beautiful song as found in Today's Wisdom.

TODAY'S WISDOM

*T*here is a place of quiet rest, near to the heart of God;
A place where sin cannot molest, near to the heart of God.

O Jesus, blest Redeemer,
Sent from the heart of God,
Hold us who wait before Thee,
Near to the heart of God.

There is a place of comfort sweet, near to the heart of God;
A place where we our Savior meet, near to the heart of God.

There is a place of full release, near to the heart of God;
A place where all is joy and peace, near to the heart of God.

Sing His Praises

———

Sing to the LORD a new song; sing to
the LORD, all the earth. Sing to the LORD, bless
His name; proclaim good tidings of His
salvation from day to day.

PSALM 96:1-2

Charles Spurgeon once said, "Stop from praising him! No never. Time may stop for it shall be no more; the world may stop, for its revolutions must cease; the universe may stop its cycles and the movings of its world, but for us to stop our songs—never, never!" Spurgeon not only knew about the power of prayer, but also the power of praise. As believers we are never to stop praising God. Our whole blessings are to be shouted from the highest mountaintop. When we stop praising, we stop receiving. The growing Christian is one who knows how to praise. Everything good comes from above, and we are to return to Him our praises.

We must consider His mercies to be "new every morning." In today's verse, the psalmist calls out for us to have a new song. He desires a new appreciation of what the Lord has done for us in the past, as well as in the present. God is still doing great things today. Look around and see the manifestations of God's handiwork. See how today's new song is revealed in nature and in humanity. Then praise the God behind each miracle of life.

It is said that when the sun is going out of sight, the Swiss herdsman of the Alps takes his alpine horn and shouts loudly through it, "Praise ye the Lord!" Then a brother herdsman on some distant slope takes up the echo, "Praise ye the Lord!" Soon another answers, still higher up the mountain, till hill shouts to hill, and peak echoes to peak the sublime anthem of praise to the Lord of all.

PRAYER

*F*ather God, let my songs reflect my praises to You. All that I have is because of Your goodness. I never want to take for granted the many blessings You bestow upon my life. Amen.

ACTION

*S*tep out with a new song. Note one new thing you have observed of God's creation.

TODAY'S WISDOM

*O*ne of the most powerful things you can do when you are weighed down with negative thoughts and emotions is to sing songs of worship to the Lord.

STORMIE OMARTIAN, *THE PRAYER THAT CHANGES EVERYTHING*

Save Time for God

Serve the LORD with gladness; come
before Him with joyful singing.

PSALM 100:2

$\mathcal{I}$n this century—even this decade—we have so many activities to distract us that weren't available to our forefathers. We also have much more leisure time to distract us from our eternal priorities. The lure away from worshiping and serving the Lord is ever increasing. We are continually being pulled away from godly priorities.

In my neighborhood I constantly see people out for walks, jogging, playing in the park, heading for the mall, going to the beach, sailing around the harbor—all good things unto themselves. But how often do activities take the place of active service or worship? Dad can even be distracted by watching sports on TV—whatever he wants to choose is available. When ESPN first announced they were going to have a 24-hour-a-day sports channel, I thought, "Who would watch that?" Boy, was I wrong. Even children's activities put a roadblock into having available time to worship and serve God.

Everyone loves the weekends. These are two days when we get to choose what we want to do. For many the activities are errands, grocery shopping, washing the car, doing laundry, cleaning the house, doing home repairs, etc. For others, Saturday and Sunday provide a break from a hard week on the job, a great time to relax, sleep in late, and have an extra cup of coffee. Yes, weekends are fun to look forward to.

Unfortunately, worship doesn't always fit into our busy weekend schedule. Because of changing values in America, attendance at our church of choice is becoming a lower and lower weekend priority for many. After the 9/11 tragedies, church attendance swelled, but now we are going back to our normal attendance. Parents can help their family recognize and heed this important weekly commitment of corporate worship. Rest assured, your children will notice the amount of importance or unimportance that Mom and Dad place on worship. If they see that God is the first one cut out of a too-busy schedule, the message they'll receive is that God is really a pretty low priority. That observation will translate into an even lesser commitment to God on their part.

But when the adults are faithful to being a vital part of a good local church, the children will notice and build a similar commitment into their own lives. The opportunity to worship God with gladness is a freedom we too often take for granted. Being at church on the weekend is a divine appointment we must strive to keep. The weekend affords us plenty of hours to do the other things we want to do, without having to skip church.

A family who delights in attending church together will share in songs of praise, prayers raised up high, the giving of tithes and offerings, and joy at hearing God's Word preached.

PRAYER

*F*ather God, I just love being in church with my family. As a mother it gives me a great sense of security having my family joining me in worship. Amen.

ACTION

*P*lan on attending weekly worship with your family.

TODAY'S WISDOM

*W*e are not blessed because we are wealthy; we are wealthy because we take time to bless.

WAYNE MULLER

Thankful Hearts Give Thanks

*Go through his open gates with great thanks-
giving; enter his courts with praise. Give thanks
to him and bless his name.*

PSALM 100:4 TLB

*G*od must think we need to be reminded to be thankful and to
give thanks, because the Book of Psalms is full of verses that remind
the reader to have a thankful heart. Dietrich Bonhoeffer wrote, "In
ordinary life we hardly realize that we receive a great deal more than
we give, and that it is only with gratitude that life becomes rich.
It is very easy to overestimate the importance of our own achieve-
ments in comparison to what we owe others."

"If only I could take a shopping cart to Target or Wal-Mart and
shop until I had all the stuff I wanted—then I would be happy!"
Have you echoed that thought before? I have a friend who often
verbalizes, "If only I could have a bigger house, a bigger car, a bigger
ring...then I would be happy." After 30 years, she is still looking for
happiness in possessions. She's looking in all the wrong places.

Thankful hearts give thanks. The Scriptures are quite clear that
a thankful heart is a happy heart. To have complete happiness, we
must enter into the Lord's presence with thanksgiving. I've found
that when I do have a spirit of thanksgiving, I am healthier emotion-
ally, spiritually, and physically. Life feels better and richer.

PRAYER

*F*ather God, I come to You in gratitude for all You have given me. Your grace is sufficient for all my needs. Thankful hearts do give thanks. Amen.

ACTION

*G*ive praise to God for all your blessings.

TODAY'S WISDOM

*O*h, Lord, I thank You for the privilege and gift of living in a world filled with beauty and excitement and variety. I thank you for the gift of loving and being loved. ...I thank you for the delights of music and children, of other men's thoughts and conversation and their books to read by the fireside or in bed with the rain falling on the roof or the snow blowing past outside the window.

LOUIS BROMFIELD

Walk with Integrity

---

*I will walk within my house in
the integrity of my heart.*

PSALM 101:2

It seems like we are living in a time when integrity is being challenged. *Webster's New World Dictionary* defines *integrity* as "the quality or state of being of sound moral principle; uprightness, honesty, and sincerity."

In order for us to walk with integrity of heart, we must possess a heart that has been molded and shaped after God's own heart. Our hearts are changed by the righteousness of God. He is the Potter; we are the clay. Let Him shape us in His own way. All throughout Scripture we are being taught about the heart:

- God looks at the heart (1 Samuel 16:7).
- Serve Him with a whole heart (1 Chronicles 28:9).
- He knows the secrets of the heart (Psalm 44:21).
- "Create in me a clean heart" (Psalm 51:10).
- "Thy word I have treasured in my heart" (Psalm 119:11).
- A joyful heart is good medicine (Proverbs 17:22).
- Love the Lord with your heart (Mark 12:30).
- With the heart man believes (Romans 10:10).
- Make melody with your heart (Ephesians 5:19).
- Draw near with a sincere heart (Hebrews 10:22).

As you can see, the heart controls the integrity of the whole body. How our heart goes, so goes our character. If we have a righteous heart, we will spread righteousness; if our hearts are impure, we aren't capable of spreading moral goodness. As sinners, we all must approach God in this fashion: "O Lord, give me a transformed heart. Make me a new person. I want to toss away the old and let a newness begin within me now."

PRAYER

*L*ord, help me make the tough decisions of life without compromising my integrity and my relationship with You. Let my heart be pure. Amen.

ACTION

*R*ead through the heart verses and think on the ways in which you can strengthen your own love for God and for His goodness.

TODAY'S WISDOM

*W*e must always remember that God has given to every soul the responsibility of deciding what its character and destiny shall be.

CHARLES JEFFERSON

Give Till It Hurts

I will bless the Lord and not forget the
glorious things he does for me.
Psalm 103:2 tlb

We take for granted so many things that happen to us, not taking the time to realize that God has His hand in what just occurred. My son Brad called this morning and said his car was heating up and had to be towed to the garage for repair. Then he shared that he had gotten home late the night before after a 300-mile trip. When he told me the last part, I shouted over the phone, "Thank You, Jesus!" His car could have broken down late at night on the freeway. So many things happen just like that. I never want to forget the glorious things God does for me and my family.

Some people say we have two arms because one arm is for receiving and the other arm is for giving. This gives us a balanced life when we can do both—giving and receiving. We don't just want to always receive. We must remember that 50 percent of the time we are to give. When I give the perfect gift to someone, I can't wait to see the expression on the person's face. There is such joy in making someone else's day. A kind word is free to give to anyone at any time, and the dividends are great.

Some of the most wonderful greeting cards I have received were handmade by my grandchildren. I set them out so all our guests could see them. Everything we have is a gift—our health, our hearing, our eyesight, our mental abilities, our jobs, our homes—each given to us by God. Why waste time reflecting on what we don't have? Let's fill our minds with the things we do have. Negative thoughts destroy; positive thoughts make us full of joy. Learn to give abundantly, and your barns will be overflowing with grain.

PRAYER

*G*od, You have given me and my family so much. In return I want to give to others. Lead me to give more. Amen.

ACTION

*B*e a joy and a blessing to someone today.

TODAY'S WISDOM

*J*esus went over to the collection boxes in the Temple and sat and watched as the crowds dropped in their money. Some who were rich put in large amounts. Then a poor widow came and dropped in two pennies. He called his disciples to him and remarked, "That poor widow has given more than all those rich men put together! For they gave a little of their extra fat, while she gave up her last penny."

MARK 12:41-44 TLB

He Is the Potter

O LORD, how many are Your works!
In wisdom You have made them all; the earth
is full of Your possessions.
PSALM 104:24

I'm writing this section of devotions as we are entering the first day of spring at our lovely southern California beach community. As I journeyed outside this morning to bring in the newspaper, I happened to see all the new creations of God: All my lovely flowers are in full bloom, the sky is beautifully blue with a few clouds flowing overhead, our white birch trees have leaves so green you would think they sprang out just for Saint Patrick's day, the salt water in the bay is as smooth as silk, not a ripple to be seen on its surface. With all this grandeur, I stood in awe to know that it was all created by God, and He is loaning it to me just for a while.

Over the years, my Bob has told me and the grandchildren stories about when he lived on a farm in Texas. Of course we all know how big Texas stories are, but this particular one has stuck in my mind because it truly exemplifies the majesty of God's abundance in creation.

As a young boy, Bob and his two brothers would go for a two-week summer vacation on their grandfather's farm in the little west Texas town of Anson to help him with the many farm chores. They would take turns riding behind a team of mules to plow the ground after tending to the weeds that grew in the furrows. They fed the animals at night, picked up the eggs for the next morning's breakfast, and picked cotton in season.

During the heat of the summer, they would get very hot and sweaty. One of their great rewards was to go to the watermelon patch and break open a ripe melon. The juice ran all over, and this sweet refreshment gave them a break from a hard day's work.

In one of his lectures, the famous American lawyer and creationist William Jennings Bryan remarked that even a watermelon speaks volumes about God's creation. "There are many questions we can ask: 'Who designed such a melon? How did the watermelon seed get so strong? How did the color and flavoring get inside the juicy melon?'"[7]

Bryan pointed out that until we can figure out the mysteries of the watermelon, how can we begin to understand the awesomeness of creation? We only have to look around us to see the power of God revealed in all He has made.

PRAYER

*F*ather God, I'm awestruck by the works of Your hands. Thank You for creating me and the world we live in. Amen.

ACTION

*T*ake a flower and study how beautiful it is and note the awesomeness of the details of the creation.

TODAY'S WISDOM

The architect can rear a cathedral, the sculptor can cut forms of symmetry and grace from marble, the painter can depict life on its canvas, the machinist can construct engines that shall serve the nations; but not one of them can create. They work with materials already in existence. They bring existing things into new combinations; this is all. God alone can create.

DR. MICHAEL GUIDO

Call Out to God

*Because He has inclined His ear to me, there-
fore I shall call upon Him as long as I live.*
PSALM 116:2

*M*ake it your priority to spend time daily with God. There's not
a single right time or one proper place. The only requirement for a
right time with God is your willing heart. Your meeting time with
God will vary according to the season of your life and the schedules
you are juggling. Jesus often slipped away to be alone in prayer
(Luke 5:16), but even His prayer times varied. He prayed in the
morning and late at night, on a hill and in the upper room.

I know people who spend hours commuting on the southern
California freeways who use that time to be with God. In my young
married life, I used to get up earlier than the rest of the family for
a quiet time of reading the Scriptures and praying. Now that the
children are raised and the home is quiet, I find morning is still
the best time for me, before the telephone starts to ring or I get
involved in the day's activities. Maybe I'm one of the odd ones,
but I enjoy arriving at church early and having 10 to 15 minutes
to open my Bible and think on God's thoughts. I use this block of
time to prepare my heart for worship. I believe if more members of
the congregation devoted time to reading Scripture and praying for
the service before the service, church would be more meaningful
for every worshiper.

Meeting alone with God each day should be a constant in our life. After all, God has made it clear that He is interested in His children (1 Peter 5:7). For many women, this is a very new and exciting part of their spiritual development, yet they are not sure what to do during their quiet time with the Lord. I suggest reading and meditating on God's Word for a while, then spending some time with Him in prayer. Talk to Him as you would to your earthly parent or to a special friend who loves you, desires the best for you, and wants to help you in every way possible.

Here are a few suggestions for your conversation with God:

- Praise God for who He is (Psalm 150).
- Thank God for all He has done for you (Philippians 4:6).
- Confess your sins (1 John 1:9).
- Pray for your family (Philippians 2:4).
- Pray for yourself (Philippians 4:6).

Time with your heavenly Father is never wasted. If you spend time alone with God in the morning, you'll start your day refreshed and ready for whatever comes your way. If you spend time alone with Him in the evening, you'll go to sleep relaxed, resting in His care and ready for a new day to serve Him.

Remember, too, that you can talk to Him anytime, anywhere: in school, at work, on the freeway, at home. You don't have to have an appointment to ask Him for something you need or to thank Him for something you have received from Him. God is interested in everything that happens to you. After all, you are His child.

PRAYER

*F*ather God, thank You for being within the sound of my voice and only a thought away. May I never forget to call on You in every situation. I want to bring before You my adoration, confession, thanksgiving, and supplication. Amen.

ACTION

*T*ell someone of your commitment to spend time daily with God in study and in prayer. Ask this person to hold you accountable.

TODAY'S WISDOM

I asked for bread and got a stone;
I used the stone to grind the grain
That made the flour to form the bread
That I could not obtain.
Instead of asking Him to give
The things for which we pray,
All that we need to ask
From God is this: Show us the way.

JAMES A. BOWMAN

Make Time for Quiet Time

*The LORD preserves the simple; I was brought
low, and He saved me.*

PSALM 116:6

As I have gotten older, I have yearned for a simpler life. I've realized that the more you have, the more that needs attention, repairs, dusting, replacement, etc. I've told our children that I don't want any more things. If it needs shelf space, dusting, or is breakable, I don't want it. Just give me consumable items like flowers, candies, lunches, gift certificates, or cruises (that would be very nice!). My quiet times with the Lord have become very precious to me. I anxiously look forward to this uplifting time I have in my prayer closet each day.

I've established a few guidelines to help you create nourishing devotions. Clutter wearies the spirit! Take at least 15 minutes to "dejunk" the room where you plan to be with God. A meaningful quiet time includes food for the soul, so keep your Bible, note cards, and a pen in a small wicker basket that becomes your prayer basket. With just a quick pickup, you can take your tools anywhere you want to meet Jesus. Today it may be in your prayer closet; tomorrow it may be in the park.

You may let this new season of quiet start by reading Ecclesiastes 3. As you read the whole chapter, you will realize that there is a time for every pursuit under the sun. Consider from that chapter what time in life it is for you. What percentage of life is still left for your inward pursuits?

Don't hesitate to take time out for quiet when everything in life gets to be too much. Set a timer for 15 minutes and disappear from the family. Let the family know that you would like not to be disturbed while you are conversing with your Lord. If you work outside the home, take a walk somewhere quiet and lovely. Drive to a park nearby. Read, pray, and return to your job refreshed. It's time to make time for quiet time, pure and simple.

PRAYER

Lord, slow me down so that I can make quiet time for You. I know that the simple life creates less stress in my life. Help me to make this a top priority for my daily schedule. Amen.

ACTION

Assemble a prayer basket for this special time.

TODAY'S WISDOM

Perhaps the greatest blessing in marriage is that it lasts so long. The years, like the varying interests of each year, combine to buttress and enrich each other. Out of many shared years, one life. In a series of temporary relationships, one misses the ripening, gathering, harvesting joys, the deep, hard-won truths of marriage.

RICHARD C. CABOT

God Will Raise You Up

This is my comfort in my affliction,
that Your word has revived me.

PSALM 119:50

$\mathscr{I}$ have lived out this verse in my own life. God's Word has played such a large part in my recovery. There were many days when His words were just the encouragement that I needed. I would read verses that reminded me of His holiness and His sovereignty:

- "The LORD within her is righteous; he does no wrong. Morning by morning he dispenses his justice, and every new day he does not fail" (Zephaniah 3:5 NIV).

- "O LORD, you are my God; I will exalt you and praise your name, for in perfect faithfulness you have done marvelous things, things planned long ago" (Isaiah 25:1 NIV).

- "We wait in hope for the LORD; he is our help and our shield" (Psalm 33:20 NIV).

- "May the LORD, the God of your fathers, increase you a thousand times and bless you as he has promised!" (Deuteronomy 1:11 NIV).

- "O Lord, you are our Father. We are the clay and you are the Potter. We are all formed by your hand" (Isaiah 64:8 TLB).

- "For everything that was written in the past was written to teach us, so that through endurance and the encouragement of the Scriptures we might have hope" (Romans 15:4 NIV).

I have found that God doesn't always lift us out of our circumstances. But He is always with us in our situation. Jesus becomes the light within our darkness. In Hebrews 11:35-38 we are told that many believers often suffer. God never promises earthly perfection, but He does promise to always stand beside us and never to forsake us (see Deuteronomy 31:6 and Hebrews 13:5). He will give us strength and the grace to rejoice while we are in those situations.

Yes, God's Word does permit us to walk through the valley of the shadow of death. "I will fear no evil; for thou art with me" (Psalm 23:4 KJV). I have tested the Scriptures, and I have been able to trust them in the past, in the present, and assuredly in the future.

PRAYER

Father God, Your Word is never-failing. It has given me hope during my darkest hour. When I felt like quitting, You lifted me up. Thank You! Amen.

ACTION

Test God's Word to see that it is true in all situations.

TODAY'S WISDOM

For none of us lives to himself alone and none of us dies to himself alone. If we live, we live to the Lord; and if we die, we die to the Lord. So, whether we live or die, we belong to the Lord.

ROMANS 14:7-8 NIV

Have an Eternal Perspective

You are my refuge and my shield, and your
promises are my only source of hope.

PSALM 119:114 TLB

$\mathcal{I}$t's amazing how divided our country is. We are split 50/50 in almost all facets of life—all the way from our political choices to the culture that we want. We can't understand how certain people think the way they do, and they can't understand the way we think. We have become a country of people who are "in your face." I used to know how people thought and the values they represent. Today I'm not sure that I do. But I look upward!

People have asked me how I can be so upbeat when so many things around me are negative. I guess it's because of my perspective on life. Through Scripture and life experiences, I have come to trust that God has a master plan for my life. He knew my beginning, and He knows the events of my end. His words give me so much comfort. I have learned that I can count on His promises. When the psalmist tells me that God is my shield and that His promises are my only source of hope, I believe it. God's character is one of honor, trust, and reliability that I can bank on for my life.

God's Word brings me light on a foggy day, it brings me hope when I become discouraged, and it helps me not to make a mountain out of a molehill. His Word gives me the right perspective on life. I know that my time on earth is so short, and my time with

Him after this earthly experience will be for eternity. I have conquered death through Christ—it has no sting; it is swallowed up in victory (1 Corinthians 15:54-56).

PRAYER

Father God, You are an eternal God. You always have been, and You always will be. I trust Your will for my life. The longer I live, the more I want to be Christlike. I appreciate Your guidance in helping me make the right choices for my life. Amen.

ACTION

Make choices today that have eternal value.

TODAY'S WISDOM

President Ulysses S. Grant (1822–1885) said:

> Hold fast to the Bible as the sheet-anchor of your liberties. Write its precepts in your hearts, and practice them in your lives. To the influence of this Book are we indebted for all the progress made in true civilization, and to this we must look as our guide in the future.

THE SUNDAY SCHOOL TIMES, 1876

Be a Woman of Praise

*Seven times a day I praise You, because of Your
righteous ordinances.*

PSALM 119:164

We have all been around people who are down in the dumps. I
met a lady the other day who seemed upset. I asked her how she was,
to which she responded, "I'm okay, considering the circumstances."
So many people let circumstances determine how they feel. As hard
as it can be, we have to choose to live above the circumstances.

Do you know a complainer? These people complain about little
things and big things. You name it, they complain. Nothing looks
good, tastes good, feels good, sounds good. No matter what happens, the hole gets deeper, and life is just not worth living. Suicide
has even crossed their minds. They think no one will miss them, and
they will certainly be happier without all the pains of life. Maybe
you have been this low before. Please know that there is great hope
and help in the Lord.

Our verse for today helps us break through the barrier of despair
because it charges us to praise God seven times a day. No one can
remain negative for very long when they are praising God for their
abundance of gifts—not just for material possessions, but also for
blessings of health, family, energy, church family, country, lay minis-
tries, nurses, doctors, hospitals, Bible teachers, coaches, policemen,
firemen, a bed to sleep in, clean sheets, a comfortable pillow, Social

Security retirement checks, vacations, and so on. There is so much for which to be thankful.

We cannot let our minds dwell on the negative when God has given us so much. Once we begin to dwell on the positive, our whole disposition will change. We begin to see beautiful sunsets rather than a cloudy, rainy sky.

Praise one time—two times—three times—four times—five times—six times—seven times a day. Yes, seven times a day will I praise the Lord.

PRAYER

*F*ather God, I want to be a woman of praise. Thanks for reminding me to think on the goodness of life. Amen.

ACTION

*P*raise God today seven times. Try to do this for a week and see how your attitude changes, even if your circumstances do not.

TODAY'S WISDOM

*F*inally, brethren, whatever is true, whatever is honorable, whatever is right, whatever is pure, whatever is lovely, whatever is of good repute, if there is any excellence and if anything worthy of praise, dwell on these things.

PHILIPPIANS 4:8

Christic the Solid Rock

My help comes from the LORD,
who made heaven and earth.

PSALM 121:2

Sometimes when I was experiencing the weakness, the despair that the cancer journey can bring, I wondered if I was going to make it. Yes, my support group encouraged me, and hundreds of prayer partners assured me by cards and letters that I was going to make it, but my mind was often plagued with negative thoughts about my future. Satan so wanted to defeat me by making me lose hope for recovery. Yet my faith remained victorious, and my daily walk with God helped me climb the many mountains put before me. The power of the Trinity was truly the rock that provided me a firm foundation.

Bill Martin Jr. tells a story of how a young Indian boy was able to overcome his fear of failure:

> "Grandfather, will I ever be strong like you?" the little
> boy asked.
> His grandfather reassured him, "You're growing stronger
> every day."

"How strong must I be, Grandfather?" the boy asked.

"You must be so strong that you will not speak with anger, even when your heart is filled with anger. You must be so strong that you will listen to what others are saying, even when your own thoughts are begging for expression. You must be so strong that you will always stop to remember what happened yesterday and foresee what will happen tomorrow so that you will know what to do today."

"Then will I be strong enough to cross over the dark mountains?" the boy asked.

The wise grandfather answered, "You already have crossed some of the dark mountains, my grandson. But these mountains of sorrow have no beginning and no ending. They are all around us. We can only know that we are crossing them when we want to be weak but choose to be strong."

When you're called to cross the dark mountains surrounding you, be brave even when you feel like being weak. Lift your face skyward and pray that God will be your rock. May He give you strength far beyond your expectations.

PRAYER

God, when I am weak, then You make me strong. You are my rock when I face a mountain that seems too vast, too scary, too unknown. You are beside me every step of the way. It is Your strength that carries me over. Amen.

ACTION

Write in your journal about your personal journey over the dark mountain.

TODAY'S WISDOM

*I*t is in the whole process of meeting and solving problems that life has meaning. Problems are the cutting edge that distinguishes between success and failure. Problems call forth our courage and our wisdom; indeed, they create our courage and our wisdom. It is only because of problems that we grow mentally and spiritually. It is through the pain of confronting and resolving problems that we learn.

M. SCOTT PECK

God's Security System

⊷⊷⊷

*The LORD will guard your going out and your
coming in from this time forth and forever.*
PSALM 121:8

*D*uring the last seven years of battling cancer (I'm presently
cancer-free), we have had times when we had to have reassurances
from our many friends that God had not forgotten us. Sometimes
it seemed like our prayers weren't being answered. Yes, our faith
was strong, and we still believed with all our hearts, but we needed
added Scripture and prayers for support.

A very energetic and self-confident older woman told her pastor,
"I don't need Jesus in the daytime while I'm awake. I can take care
of myself. But I do pray at night for when I'm asleep. In fact, I've
said bedtime prayers since I was a child."

I know a lot of people who seem more than capable of taking
care of themselves during the light of day, but they aren't quite as
confident when the sun sets. During this season of illness, I can tell
you that I have experienced prayer needs 24 hours a day, 7 days
a week, 52 weeks a year. It is so reassuring to know that the Lord
preserves us while we go out and when we come in. God's protection covers us at all times. He has a great security system around
His children. It's so comforting to know that nothing happens to
us that isn't first run by God. Only those incidents that are for my
good get by Him.

Truly all things work together for good to those who love God, to those who are called according to His purpose (Romans 8:28).

PRAYER

*L*ord and Protector, how awesome You are to know and care about all my needs. I thank You for watching out for me when I go out and when I come in. Amen.

ACTION

*S*tep out today and trust God for the little things of life.

TODAY'S WISDOM

*C*ancer is so limited...
It cannot cripple Love
It cannot shatter Hope
It cannot corrode Faith
It cannot destroy Peace
It cannot kill Friendship
It cannot suppress Memories
It cannot silence Courage
It cannot invade the Soul
It cannot steal Eternal Life
It cannot conquer the Spirit

AUTHOR UNKNOWN

A Place Called Home

Unless the LORD builds the house, they
labor in vain who build it.
PSALM 127:1

$\mathscr{A}$fter watching his house burn down, a small boy was quoted as saying, "We still have a home; we just don't have a house to put it in." How perceptive. This child knew that a home is different from a house. It is more than wood and concrete. But how does one make a house into a home?

With the fullness of today's lifestyle, our home can seem like a stopover place to eat, do laundry, hang around, and sleep. But a true home is much more than all that. It is a place of people living, growing, dying, laughing, crying, learning, and creating together.

Our home should be a place where the entire family can grow, make mistakes, laugh, cry, agree, and disagree. Home should be a place where happy experiences occur—a shelter from the problems of the world and a place of love, acceptance, and security. When we read the morning newspaper, we are confronted with all the tragedies around us. We realize that the world outside our front door is falling apart, but within our four walls we can offer a place called home.

Even though God designed marriage, family, and home to be a permanent relationship, this isn't automatic. In our key verse for today we read, "Unless the LORD builds the house, its builders labor in vain" (NIV). God is not only the designer, but He also wants to occupy the headship of family life. He wants to guide and to give love, peace, and forgiveness abundantly.

With Jesus as Lord of your family, you can have a happy home. If you yield to Him daily, your home can be a place of growing and learning together with God.

PRAYER

*F*ather, my heart's desire is to have a home rather than just a house. I want Your love to always be present. Give me the strength and courage to make the personal sacrifices necessary to transform my four walls into a home! Amen.

ACTION

*P*ray for your home and its various members. Pray for those who visit.

TODAY'S WISDOM

A home is...filled with fragrant and appealing spiritual riches when each member adopts a servant's spirit. Most family arguments and dissension stem from a failure to yield personal rights. A person filled with the Spirit of Christ strongly desires to serve. He does not seek to establish his own emotional turf but freely edifies and encourages other family members through his servant spirit.

CHARLES STANLEY

Learning to Wait

—◦—

I wait for the LORD, my soul waits, and in his
word I put my hope. My soul waits for the Lord
more than watchmen wait for the morning.
PSALM 130:5-6 NIV

When I was a child, my parents would tell me to wait until Saturday, wait until Christmas, wait until Dad comes home, or wait until I was older. It was always "Wait. Wait." I found this to be one of the hardest words to hear. In John 11:6, Mary and Martha had sent for Jesus to return home because their brother, Lazarus, was sick and near death. But Jesus waited two days before He returned to Judea. I'm sure that they must have asked the question, "Where is God when I need Him?" Throughout Scripture we are told to wait and be patient:

- "Blessed are all those who wait for him to help them" (Isaiah 30:18 TLB).
- "Don't be impatient. Wait for the Lord, and he will come and save you....Yes, wait and he will help you" (Psalm 27:14 TLB).
- "It is better to be patient than powerful" (Proverbs 16:32 NLT).
- "A patient man has great understanding" (Proverbs 14:29 NIV).
- "Be glad for all God is planning for you. Be patient in trouble, and always be prayerful" (Romans 12:12 NLT).

During my years of treatment for cancer, the waiting was one of the most difficult aspects. Waiting is a struggle for most people. When things are going well, we wait for them to get better. When times are hard, we wait for circumstances to improve. We wait for good things in anticipation and frustration. And when we are ill or in trouble, the waiting can be more excruciating. We should not be surprised that so many passages in the Bible speak about enduring and being patient. Jesus said that in this world we would have trouble. He didn't specifically add that a lot of our trouble would involve waiting.

Why is waiting so hard? Sometimes we're in a hurry because we want the outcome so badly. We just have to know. Another reason waiting is so hard is that it takes away our illusion of control. Our spirits rebel against this reminder that our time and agenda are not our own. A lot of life is outside of our power and control.

When we faithfully endure, we develop the character and virtue of waiting. I found that the more I learned from waiting, the stronger my faith became. Have you ever experienced that time of perseverance and growth? One of the greatest lessons we can learn is that God does not abandon us, He does not forsake us, and when we are waiting for answers, change, healing, and hope, He is with us.

PRAYER

God, let me use this waiting time to develop my trust in You. I don't have to know all the answers just now. I can wait upon Your revelations. Amen.

ACTION

Wait, wait, wait.

TODAY'S WISDOM

*P*atience is more than endurance. A saint's life is in the hands of God like a bow and arrow in the hands of an archer. God is aiming at something the saint cannot see, and He stretches and strains, and every now and again the saint says—"I cannot stand any more." God does not heed, He goes on stretching till His purpose is in sight, then He lets fly. Trust yourself in God's hands. For what have you need of patience just now? Maintain your relationship to Jesus Christ by the patience of faith. "Though He slay me, yet will I wait for Him."

OSWALD CHAMBERS

Be a Humble Servant of God

———

*O LORD, my heart is not proud, nor my eyes
haughty; nor do I involve myself in great matters, or in things too difficult for me.*

PSALM 131:1

David the psalmist urgently cries out in his despair for the Lord
to hear his prayer for forgiveness. His sins overwhelm him, and he
feels as though he is drowning. All through the Psalms, David has
pleaded with God for His forgiveness. Time and time again, David
offers such a prayer of humility and trust. He desperately wants
God's gift of forgiveness.

God forgives, and David's gratitude for God's grace leads him
to reverent fear and obedience. He urges other people to wait confidently and expectantly for God. How easy or difficult is this for
you to do? When we are seeking God's forgiveness, we must have
a quiet heart and peace within. We must confess our sins and be
removed from the heavy weight of conviction. We can trust in the
Lord's love and compassion now and forevermore.

In this verse, we can see a peace that David has. He is not speaking
as a king or a warrior but as a humble, broken man who has turned
from his self-centered pride and arrogance. He no longer is caught
up with glorious titles, with authority to negotiate the big deals of
the day. Instead he is content and at peace with his status in life.

We live in a very wealthy part of southern California with magnificent homes, private jets, expensive yachts, private schools, on and on. Orange County reflects the prime real estate along our beautiful coastline. Through our church we continually hear of corporate executives who have lived the fast track, but now have turned their backs on all this grandeur. They no longer strive for the titles, the wealth, or the popularity. Many have resigned from the ivory tower so they can spend more time with their families. David knew what it was like to have everything. Now he was satisfied with a slower, less complicated life. He wanted to be God's man.

PRAYER

*F*ather, I have never been to the heights of David. My life is so simple compared to his, but I thank You for my simple trust and faith. These virtues have been a blessing to me and my family. Amen.

ACTION

*G*o to the Lord and cleanse yourself of all unrighteousness.

TODAY'S WISDOM

*A*s the prince or ruler only has power to pardon treason in his subjects, so God only has power to forgive sin. As no man can forgive a debt but the creditor to whom the debt is due, so God only can forgive us our debts, whose debtors we are to an incalculable amount.

AUTHOR UNKNOWN

Be Positive in Thought

How precious it is, Lord, to realize
that you are thinking about me constantly!
I can't even count how many times a day your
thoughts turn towards me.

PSALM 139:17

*R*ecently I read a report which stated that most women have difficulty in accepting who they are. Their nose is too large, their chin is recessed, their ears stick out too far, their weight is out-of-control, etc. There is a tremendous increase in the number of cosmetic surgeries taking place in America. Women are the main patients, but men are getting in on the make-over action as well. Shows like "Extreme Makeovers" have been a big hit in the reality craze. It seems like very few of us are satisfied with the "me" God created.

Do you ever catch your thoughts taking a negative turn when you consider your value? Most of us are very good at criticizing ourselves. We find fault very easily. I suggest that you develop a positive, healthy thought process: "I know that God is thinking about me constantly, how can I not think positively of myself? If I am worthy to Him, why should I not be worthy to myself?"

As we look in the mirror of life, however, we must recognize that all good comes from our heavenly Father. He thinks about us continually. He wants us to be successful in life. Let's make lemonade out of our lemons. Following God's lead of turning difficulties into times of rejoicing, my Bob and I would go out and celebrate after

I finished delicate medical procedures. Usually we didn't do anything big—just a recognition that I had done a "good job." Keep telling yourself the positive. Don't let the negative take hold of your thought process. Remember, each time you tear yourself down, you are criticizing a person God made, God loves, and God cares for.

PRAYER

*F*ather God, keep negative thoughts from entering my mind. I want them out of my life. I don't want to waste positive energy on negative thoughts. I'm made in Your image. Help me believe this completely and give You praise for this special person You made—me! Amen.

ACTION

*W*hen those thoughts creep into your mind and heart, say, "Negative thoughts, get behind me."

TODAY'S WISDOM

A new day rose upon me. It was as if another sun had risen into the sky; the heavens were indescribably brighter, and the earth fairer; and that day has gone on brightening to the present hour. I have known the other joys of life, I suppose, as much as most men; I have known art and beauty, music and gladness; I have known friendship and love and family ties; but it is certain that till we see God in the world—God in the bright and boundless universe—we never know the highest joy. It is far more than if one were translated to a world a thousand times fairer than this; for that supreme and central Light of Infinite Love and Wisdom, shining over this world and all worlds, alone can show us how noble and beautiful, how fair and glorious they are.

Orville Dewey

Does Anyone Care?

—◁▭◦▭▷—

Look to the right and see; for there is
no one who regards me; there is no escape for
me; no one cares for my soul.

PSALM 142:4

*W*ith increasing teenage and college-age suicides, we hear the cry, "No one cares for me! No one!" A white-collar worker in a towering office building goes bankrupt. Who cares? A punch-press operator in a sprawling factory dies in a rush-hour traffic accident. Who cares? A teenager is shot by a drive-by shooter and dies. Who cares?

We live in an age when depersonalization, estrangement, isolation, and loneliness are rampant. We tend to go right along with the crowd by pretending we're content. But inside, many of us feel desperately alone. We join clubs, groups, organizations, and churches to find our place. These are healthy choices, but even with all this joining, many people still feel unloved and lonely.

Beneath our facade of coolness, we struggle with doubts, lingering fears, and paralyzing anxieties. We stay silent, but secretly hope for someone to come along who will listen, who will care, and who will understand. Many of us ask with the psalmist who wrote today's verse, "Does anyone care for my soul?" Jesus says in Mark 8:36 (NKJV), "What will it profit a man if he gains the whole world, and loses his own soul?" Here is someone who cares because He recognizes the worth of one single soul. Jesus cares! He is also

194

the One who states, "Are not two sparrows sold for a copper coin? And not one of them falls to the ground apart from your Father's will. But the very hairs of your head are all numbered. Do not fear therefore; you are of more value than many sparrows" (Matthew 10:29-31 NKJV).

To accept Jesus' love is to find real peace and the assurance of true belonging. He "will never leave you nor forsake you" (Hebrews 13:5 NKJV).

PRAYER

*F*ather, I thank You for caring for me. Your love has given me hope and assurance for today. May I pass that hope on to someone else today. Amen.

ACTION

*S*hare with someone today that you care.

TODAY'S WISDOM

*I*n Christ, there is freedom from bondage. Believers are no longer slaves; they are free—not through their own merit but through God's redeeming grace.

RHONDA H. KELLEY

Step Out of the Box

Teach me to do Your will, for You are my God;
let Your good Spirit lead me on level ground.
PSALM 143:10

The chief purpose of man is to know God and to enjoy Him forever. One of the ways that I get to enjoy God is to enjoy His creation and all of His creativity. Did you know that creativity isn't just for self-fulfillment? Much of the joy is in sharing it with other people. In fact, the Book of Genesis tells us that God created human beings in order to have fellowship. His creative handiwork produced a beautiful garden home for the first man and woman. His heart was to bless them with its creative glory!

We first learned this truth as children, as we crayoned master-pieces for people we loved. The real joy came in running to Mommy and Daddy to share our handiwork. It even got better when our masterpiece appeared on the front of the refrigerator. Our son went one step farther when he framed his children's artwork and hung it on the walls throughout their home. The children's artwork became his treasured art collection.

We still experience the joy of creating and sharing when we cross-stitch a Scripture verse for a friend, or when we write up a recipe for a new acquaintance who just loved the scones we served over tea.

Once when I was recovering from surgery, a dear friend came

to my hospital room with a "recovery kit." In a pretty basket she'd wrapped gifts labeled Day One, Day Two, and so on. She had a gift a day for 12 consecutive days. Each day I opened a special gift: a sweet card, a refrigerator magnet, a little puzzle, a can of chicken soup, a candle, a jar of spa cream, etc.

The simple gift of creativity is really the gift of ourselves.

PRAYER

*C*reator, I love Your thoughts and actions for their creativity. I want those juices to run throughout my body. Let me see beyond myself and look to nature for my inspiration. Amen.

ACTION

*B*reak out of your routine today. Give yourself permission to be creative.

TODAY'S WISDOM

*Y*our success as family, our success as a society, depends not on what happens in the White House, but on what happens inside your house.

BARBARA BUSH

Share a Meal Together

*The eyes of all look to You, and You give
them their food in due time.*

PSALM 145:15

*O*ne of the great traditions of yesteryear that returned great dividends to the family was to have dinner/supper together. A leading university recently did research to study what successful families have in common. Time and time again the participants responded, "We had the evening meal together." Any of us who grew up with this tradition or are making it a tradition in our homes already understand the value of coming to the table together as a family.

I long for the good old days, when our family gathered every night over a meal and shared events of the day. Life seemed a lot less busy then, and there weren't so many options to keep us away from the house or the table. It's sad for me to see family meals becoming a thing of the past for so many.

Tonight, buck the trend. Plan a memorable mealtime with family. Set the table with extras that will make every family member feel special and celebrated. Candles, placemats, tablecloths, and a simple, low centerpiece of flower sprigs or fruit create a spirit of warmth at mealtime. Obviously, food takes the starring role, so healthy, tasty fare is best. Ask your family to list some of their favorite meal entrées and select a day of the week that showcases one of these choices.

Think of Jesus and how He chose to share a special meal with His 12 disciples during His final hours. The fellowship with these dearest of earthly companions must have given Him great comfort as He prepared for the trials ahead. Your table at home will be the gathering place for your most beloved earthly companions and will offer nourishment, both physical and spiritual, for all who join in.

Make the most of these times. They are times to cherish! They nurture more than the body; they feed the soul and prepare us for living full, productive lives.

PRAYER

*F*ather God, You have satisfied my soul. You are the One I turn to for joy, peace, and pardon. Amen.

ACTION

*S*chedule an evening with your family when you can all be together for a meal. Invite each person to talk about his or her day.

TODAY'S WISDOM

*S*he always made home happy.

EPITAPH IN A COURTYARD,
INSCRIBED BY A HUSBAND AFTER 60 YEARS OF WEDDED LIFE

Be a Woman of Thanksgiving

*I will praise the LORD while I live; I will sing
praises to my God while I have my being.*

PSALM 146:2

$\mathcal{D}$uring my recent struggle with cancer, I claimed John 11:4 as our praise verse: "This sickness is not to end in death, but for the glory of God, so that the Son of God may be glorified by it." Bob and I were determined that whatever God's will was for our lives, we were going to bring glory to Him and to His Son, Jesus.

Wherever we go, we share about God's faithfulness to us through this difficult period of our lives. Where some people might be inclined to curse God for an illness or difficult situation, we have decided to take the higher ground and praise God for all of His goodness. We are also aware that a heart of praise heals, while a heart of anger shortens a person's life.

Praise always gives peace and rest to the believer. Some of the most peaceful people I know are the ones with the most pain. Why? Because they are aware of the healing that takes place with glorifying the Lord. Does praise always bring healing? No! But it does bring peace and comfort during the process.

Many of our friends have shared how we have modeled for them how to praise God. How you respond when times become difficult can be such a witness to other people. Don't wait until a crisis arrives in your life (I guarantee that it will) to glorify God, but begin now to praise Him. When that day arrives (and it surely will), you will have Scripture already in your heart to see you through your journey of difficulties.

Throughout the Psalms, we read how the various writers come to one of the basic principles for living a balanced Christian life: We are to "praise the Lord." When we rise past the hurts and disappointments in life, we dramatically shout, "Praise the Lord!" Often in our youth and when life is going great, we tend to forget all that God does for us. Prepare for tomorrow by praising God today.

PRAYER

*L*ord, thank You for all Your blessings in my life. I can never repay You for Your faithfulness. Even during my hardest times, You are there to lean on, guide me, lift me out of my despair, and guard my heart. I praise You for all You are. Amen.

ACTION

*I*n your own way, praise the Lord today.

TODAY'S WISDOM

*T*hank God for…
   …your talents and abilities by investing them in goodness.
   …the opportunities He has given you by giving opportunities to other people.
   …your happiness by striving to make others happy.
   …the beauty of life by making the world more beautiful.
   …inspiration by being an inspiration to others.
   …your good health by respecting and taking care of your own body.
   …each new day by living it to the fullest.

Share Your Load

---

*He lifts the burdens from those bent
down beneath their loads. For the
Lord loves good men.*

PSALM 146:8 TLB

I have a friend who always gives me the same answer when I ask her, "How are you doing today?" Her reply is always, "Okay, under the circumstances." Some people always want to carry their own burdens. Every situation has its own burdens, and we are told to share our burdens.

As you start a new day, do you ever think about what God's new morning message might be to us? Regardless of what our circumstance might be like, His message is always the same. Our weather might be sunny, rainy, snowy, or chilly. He always gives us the same promise. His promise is that the dawn will come at the beginning of each day. In all our troubles, He promises to be with us and to lift the burdens from our bent backs.

He wants to tell us that He will be alongside us to give support throughout the day. He hasn't forgotten us. He knows our names. He understands our circumstances. He hears our every prayer. The dawn brings a new day that contains the same promises from yesterday. Even during the darkness of night, God is there.

When you feel the weight of sorrow or loss or worry, remember that God has strong shoulders. Don't hesitate to give some of your heavy burdens to Him. In fact, He will carry all of them if you'll only give them to Him.

PRAYER

*F*ather, I love the assurance that You are with me each day. In every situation, You keep Your promises. I'm so glad You help me with today's load. Amen.

ACTION

*S*top bending over with your heavy load. Transfer the burden to Him.

TODAY'S WISDOM

*B*lessed are those whose strength is in you, who have set their hearts on pilgrimage. As they pass through the Valley of Baca, they make it a place of springs; the autumn rains also cover it with pools. They go from strength to strength, till each appears before God in Zion....For the LORD God is a sun and shield; the LORD bestows favor and honor; no good thing does he withhold from those whose walk is blameless. O LORD Almighty, blessed is the [one] who trusts in you.

PSALM 84:5-7,11-12 NIV

Notes

━━◀▮▮▯▮▮▶━━

1. Adapted from Emilie Barnes, *Cup of Hope* (Eugene, OR: Harvest House Publishers, 2000), pp. 27-29.

2. Taken from Emilie Barnes, *15 Minutes Alone with God* (Eugene, OR: Harvest House Publishers, 1994), pp. 104-06.

3. Bill Bright, "Four Spiritual Laws" (Arrowhead Springs, CA: Campus Crusade for Christ International, 1965).

4. Bob and Emilie Barnes, *15-Minute Devotions for Couples* (Eugene, OR: Harvest House Publishers, 1995), p. 84.

5. Kenneth W. Osbeck, *Compilation, Amazing Grace: 366 Hymn Stories for Personal Devotions* (Grand Rapids, MI: Kregel Publications, 1990), p. 209.

6. Osbeck, *Amazing Grace,* p. 170.

7. William Jennings Bryan, *In His Image,* chapter 1, 1922, Project Gutenberg Ebook.

Harvest House Books
by Bob & Emilie Barnes

Bob & Emilie Barnes

15-Minute Devotions
for Couples

101 Ways to Love Your
Grandkids

Abundance of the Heart

A Little Book of Manners
for Boys

Minute Meditations
for Couples

Bob Barnes

15 Minutes Alone
with God for Men

500 Handy Hints for
Every Husband

Men Under Construction

Minute Meditations for Men

Emilie Barnes

The 15-Minute Organizer

15 Minutes Alone with God

15 Minutes of Peace
with God

15 Minutes with God
for Grandma

500 Time-Saving Hints
for Women

Cleaning Up the Clutter

Emilie's Creative
Home Organizer

Everything I Know
I Learned in My Garden

Everything I Know
I Learned over Tea

Friendship Teas to Go

A Grandma
Is a Gift from God

Home Warming

If Teacups Could Talk

I Need Your Strength, Lord

An Invitation to Tea

Join Me for Tea

Keep It Simple
for Busy Women

Let's Have a Tea Party!

A Little Book of Manners

Meet Me Where I Am, Lord

Minute Meditations
for Busy Moms

Minute Meditations for Healing
and Hope

More Faith in My Day

More Hours in My Day

Quiet Moments for
a Busy Mom's Soul

A Quiet Refuge

Simple Secrets to
a Beautiful Home

Strength for Today,
Bright Hope for Tomorrow

A Tea to Comfort Your Soul

The Twelve Teas®
of Celebration

The Twelve Teas®
of Friendship